THE LIVING LAW

The Honourable Justice J.O. Pedro

authorHOUSE

AuthorHouse™
1663 Liberty Drive
Bloomington, IN 47403
www.authorhouse.com
Phone: 1 (800) 839-8640

© 2018 The Honourable Justice J.O. Pedro. All rights reserved.

No part of this book may be reproduced, stored in a retrieval system, or transmitted by any means without the written permission of the author.

Published by AuthorHouse 10/24/2018

ISBN: 978-1-5462-5784-4 (sc)
978-1-5462-5785-1 (hc)
978-1-5462-5783-7 (e)

Library of Congress Control Number: 2018910300

Print information available on the last page.

Any people depicted in stock imagery provided by Getty Images are models, and such images are being used for illustrative purposes only.
Certain stock imagery © Getty Images.

This book is printed on acid-free paper.

Because of the dynamic nature of the Internet, any web addresses or links contained in this book may have changed since publication and may no longer be valid. The views expressed in this work are solely those of the author and do not necessarily reflect the views of the publisher, and the publisher hereby disclaims any responsibility for them.

TABLE OF CONTENTS

Dedication vii
Foreword ix
Preface... xi
Acknowledgements xiii
Justices of the Supreme Court.. xv

Chapter 1
- Rule of Law and Natural Justice 1

Chapter 2
- Duty of Counsel to the Court and Society 39

Chapter 3
- Role of the Court in Society 57

Chapter 4
- Corruption and Electoral Matters 87

Chapter 5
- Construction and Interpretation 93

Chapter 6
- Jurisdiction 99

Chapter 7
- Evidence 107

Chapter 8
- Rules and Discretion of Court 111

Chapter 9
- Equity and Justice 115

Chapter 10
- Supremacy of the Constitution 149

Chapter 11
- The Executive and the Rule of Law 157

Chapter 12
- The Supreme Court and the Advancement of the Law 163

Chapter 13
- Miscellany 167

List of Cases in Alphabetical Order 179
Index 211
About the Author 215

DEDICATION

This work is dedicated to the Almighty God, whose mercy and grace has been with me throughout my life, and to my late father, who taught me that the best kind of knowledge is that which is learned for its own sake. It is also dedicated to my husband for being the most loving and supportive person in my life.

FOREWORD

I feel honoured to have been asked to write a foreword to this book. *The Living Law* is a compendium of pronouncements of eminent jurists of the appellate courts in Nigeria—pronouncements which have stood the test of time and helped in no small measure to guide the application of substantive and procedural law. Some of the dicta have been selected for the elegance of the prose employed; others, for the profound interpretation of the law in decisions that have become the locus classicus in particular areas of the law.

The compendium covers a wide range of pronouncements on law and procedure such as the weighty issue of jurisdiction, the topical issue of the rule of law and natural justice, the role of courts in the society, electoral matters, and the law of evidence. *The Living Law* is a unique and practical way of introducing the reader to judicial pronouncements. It whets the appetite and encourages a more detailed foray into the decisions in which the pronouncements were made.

The Honourable Justice Jumoke Pedro has exhibited a lot of industry in producing this work. The painstaking research carried out alongside her hectic schedule as a judge of the High Court of Lagos State, arguably the busiest State judiciary in the country, is quite commendable. It is a reflection of the author's penchant for hard work and diligence.

I recommend *The Living Law* to students, legal practitioners, law teachers, and jurists. It is laid out well and is easy to read.

I congratulate Hon. Justice Pedro for a job well done, and I look forward to reading more of her scholarly efforts in the future.

> The Honourable Justice Kudirat M.O. Kekere-Ekun
> Justice, Supreme Court of Nigeria

PREFACE

The Living Law is a compilation of notable and salient pronouncements drawn from the decisions of the Honourable Justices of the Nigerian Supreme Court and the Court of Appeal. It brings together fundamental and visionary pronouncements made by various justices of these Superior Courts of Record which are founded on the tripod of justice, rule of law, and fundamental rights in the Nigerian society.

The men who sit in the most exalted seat of justice are responsible for interpreting and construing the law of the land. They contribute towards the development of the law with a vision of laying down principles and doctrines to shape the Nigerian society. From their oracle have emanated wise and witty statements that withstand the test of time, continuously shaping and guiding the lives of the Nigerian people. These pronouncements drive societal principles and norms fundamental to the existence of society from the pivotal viewpoint of constitutionalism, equity and justice, fundamental rights, fair hearing, and societal norms and values.

It is almost needless to state that these pronouncements have guided and continue to guide and shape our lives and the legal profession, the members of which are ministers in the temple of justice. The title *The Living Law* is born of this spirit of keeping the law alive. To encourage and inspire society at large, it has been my intention to inscribe these words figuratively on marble for posterity and the guidance of future generations.

It is my sincere wish that this compilation be of immense relevance to the bench, the bar, law students, and members of the Nigerian society. I hope that the principles set forth may be gleaned at a glance, just as the Honourable Justices adopted simplicity of style in laying down these principles.

The Living Law also serves as a reference work in providing citations of the cases from which the notable pronouncements are drawn.

The Honourable Justice J. O. Pedro

ACKNOWLEDGEMENTS

I wish to acknowledge all those who have worked with me in ensuring that this book becomes a reality. In particular I wish to mention my former Judicial Assistant Eric Otojahi who worked tirelessly with me.

I wish to appreciate and thank My Lord Justice of the Supreme Court, The Hon Justice Kudirat M. O. Kekere-ekun for her contributions towards making sure that this book becomes a reality. His Lordship was about to go on annual vacation when I gave her the manuscript to write a foreword. I was surprised that not only did His Lordship go through the manuscript within a short period of time she also made several suggestions on how to move forward. I am grateful to His Lordship for writing the foreword.

I wish to thank my Lords Justices of the Supreme Court of Nigeria and Justices of the Court of Appeal who have inspired me to write this book. May the Lord continue to inspire them so that our laws can continue to develop through their notable pronouncements.

I find that these notable pronouncements have brought into foray judicial exposition of our laws and contributed immensely to the development of the Nigeria Legal system. These pronouncements have also reminded us that no nation can thrive without the Rule of law.

JUSTICES OF THE SUPREME COURT

THE HONOURABLE JUSTICE WALTER SAMUEL, NKANU ONNOGHEN, *(CHIEF JUSTICE OF NIGERIA)*

THE HONOURABLE JUSTICE IBRAHIM TANKO MUHAMMAD

THE HONOURABLE JUSTICE BODE RHODES-VIVOUR

THE HONOURABLE JUSTICE NWALI SYLVESTER NGWUTA

THE HONOURABLE JUSTICE MARY UKAEGO PETER-ODILI

THE HONOURABLE JUSTICE OLUKAYODE ARIWOOLA

THE HONOURABLE JUSTICE MUSA DATTIJO MUHAMMAD

THE HONOURABLE JUSTICE CLARA BATA OGUNBIYI

THE HONOURABLE JUSTICE KUMAI BAYANG AKA'AHS

THE HONOURABLE JUSTICE KUDIRAT MOTONMORI OLATOKUNBO KEKERE-EKUN

THE HONOURABLE JUSTICE JOHN INYANG OKORO

THE HONOURABLE JUSTICE CHIMA CENTUS NWEZE

THE HONOURABLE JUSTICE AMIRU SANUSI

THE HONOURABLE JUSTICE EJEMBI EKO

THE HONOURABLE JUSTICE AMINA ADAMU AUGIE

THE HONOURABLE JUSTICE SIDI DAUDA BAGE

THE HONOURABLE JUSTICE PAUL ADAMU GALINJE

1 RULE OF LAW AND NATURAL JUSTICE

"The essence of the rule of law is that it should never operate under the rule of force or fear. To use force to effect an act and while under the Marshall of that force, seek the court's equity, is an attempt to infuse timidity into court and operate a sabotage of the cherished rule of law. It must never be."
Kayode Eso, J.S.C.[1]

"In the area where rule of law operates, the rule of self help by force is abandoned. Nigeria being one of the countries in the world-even in the third world-which proclaim loudly to follow the rule of law, there is no room for the rule of self-help to operate. Once a dispute has arisen between a person and the government or authority and the dispute has been brought before the court, thereby invoking the judicial powers of the state, it is the duty of the government to allow the law to take its course or allow the legal and judicial process to run its full course…"
Andrews Otutu Obaseki, J.S.C.[2]

"It would be contrary to public interest that justice should be shackled by rules of procedure when the shackles will fall to the ground the moment the uncontested facts appear…"
Akintola Olufemi Ejiwunmi, J.C.A.[3]

"…ours, as the judex is to declare the law and insist that the rule of law, as opposed to the undemocratic whims and caprices of a few in the political party, must prevail".
Ejembi Eko, J.S.C.[4]

---

[1] Governor of Lagos State v. Ojukwu (1986) 1 NWLR (Pt.18) 621 at 634, F
[2] Governor of Lagos State v. Ojukwu (1986) 1 NWLR (Pt.18) 621 at 636, C-D
[3] Ogoja L.G. A. v. Offoboche (1996) 7 NWLR (Pt.458) 48 at 87F quoting Karibi-Whyte, J.S.C. in Egbe v. Adefarasin (1985) 1 NWLR (Pt.3) 549 at 569
[4] Lau v P.D.P 4 NWLR (2018) 6 NWLR (Pt.1608) 60 at 128, H-A

"My noble Lord, law is meant to provide peace, security, protection, concord and purposeful co-existence amongst citizens. No reasonable society will encourage resort to self-help for whatever reason and not certainly on mere suspicion."
Ibrahim Tanko Muhammad, J.S.C.[5]

"My Lords, I thought I should perhaps further reiterate that in this country governed according to the law and democratic norms, the law is no respecter of persons and frowns at every affront to and infractions of the rule of law once proved. It abhors impunity in whatever disguise."
Biobele Abraham Georgewill J.C.A.[6]

"it is my view that democracy thrives more on obeying and promoting the rule of law rather than the whims and caprices of the leaders against the led"
Biobele Abraham Geogewill J.C.A.[7]

"The trial Judge must be reminded that justice is only meaningful where it is done within the parameters of laid down rules and not based on the whims and caprices of individual judges."
Ita George Mbaba, J.C.A.[8]

"No Judge can form his opinion as to the frontiers of Bill of Rights in any democracy and import his pet ideas in the construction of provisions which are clear and obvious in terms of vindicating the freedoms of the individual in society."
Niki Tobi, J.C.A.[9]

---

[5] Spiess v. Oni (2016) 14 NWLR (Pt.1532) at 275, B
[6] Bello v. Governor of Gombe State (2016) 8 NWLR (Pt.1514) 219 at 291-292 G-C
[7] Okafor v. Lagos State Government (2017) 4 NWLR (Pt.1556) 404 at 442 C-D
[8] Jamin Systems Consultants Ltd v. Braithwaite (1996) 5 NWLR (Pt.449) 459 at 470, B-C
[9] Onwo v. Oko (1996) 6 NWLR (Pt.456) 584 at 613, E

"Legal technicalities should not and must not be allowed to defeat the course of justice."

Aloysius Iyorgyer Katsina-Alu, J.C.A.[10]

"The law of nature is a dictate of reason which points out an act according as it is or is not in conformity with rational. Nature has a quality of moral baseness or moral necessity and that in consequence, such an act is either forbidden or enjoined by the author of nature - God."

Ignatius Chukwudi Pats-Acholonu, J.C.A.[11]

"It is contrary to the rule of law to resort to self-help particularly when parties have handed in their dispute to the court for settlement… It is an ill wind which blows no one any good. It is against the norm of civilised behaviour and ought always to be discouraged."

Samson Odemwingie Uwaifo, J.C.A.[12]

"The now famous biblical wise and sound judgment passed by King Solomon between warring mothers; each claiming to be the mother of the child who was alive when the second child was dead, should be able to afford a lesson and good solution … generally in matters where the paramount interest of the children of a controversial marriage is called for determination. Either of the two parents would rather not have the child slaughtered and should have opted that the child be preserved, hoping that

---

[10] Ichi v. State (1996) 9 NWLR (Pt.470) 83 at 90, H
[11] Edet v. Chief of Air Staff (1994) 2 NWLR (Pt.324) 41 at 61, B quoting Grotius, the great philosopher jurist.
[12] Odogwu v. Odogwu (1994) 1 NWLR (Pt.323) 708 at 713, G-C

when the child grows up, the child would find the mother and the mother would have the child."
Ibrahim Kolapo Sulu-Gambari, J.C.A.[13]

"In the exercise of its judicial powers a court of law should adhere to constitutionality. It should not condone the commission by a State of constitutional wrong nor should it be an accessory after the fact to the commission of unconstitutionality."
George Adesola Oguntade, J.C.A.[14]

"…it is my well considered view that the courts will not entertain any rule or rules of native law and custom which will sentence a community to perpetual penury, servitude and make them social pariah."
Raphael Olufemi Rowland, J.C.A.[15]

"Both the Judge and counsel are involved in the administration of justice and as such are indispensable and viable partners in progress. They both are out to uphold the rule of law."
Niki Tobi, J.C.A.[16]

"A judgment sending a man to the gallows, must be seen to be the product of logical thinking, based upon admissible evidence, in which the facts leading to his conviction are clearly found and the legal deductions therefrom carefully made. It cannot be allowed to stand if founded upon scraggy reasoning or a

---

[13] Odogwu v. Odogwu (1994) 1 NWLR (Pt.323) 708 at 716, D-E
[14] Akaide v. State (1996) 8 NWLR (Pt.468) 525 at 531, D-E quoting Mohammed Bello, CJN in Engineering Enterprise v. A.-G., Kaduna State (1987) 2 NWLR (Pt. 57) 381 at 391.
[15] Akpalakpa v. Igbaibo (1996) 8 NWLR (Pt.468) 533 at 550, C
[16] Orakwute v. Agagwu (996) 8 NWLR (Pt.466) 359 at 376, B-C

perfunctory performance. It is so in all cases and more so in criminal cases and particularly more so in capital offences."
Owolabi Kolawole, J.C.A.[17]

"Because parties in litigation are very much aware of the almighty powers of the Constitution, they request the courts at the slightest turn in the adjudication process to invoke the supremacy provisions of section 1 of the Constitution. They like it. Some indulge in it too. But the courts of the land cannot allow parties in the judicial process to push them to invoke the supremacy provisions of the Constitution by merely raking up conflict situation where none really exists."
Niki Tobi, J.C.A.[18]

"The day should never come when the scope of the jurisdiction of the Judge to decide a matter is to be circumscribed by the legal erudition of learned counsel. It is strange to say that the judge cannot apply principles not referred to by counsel. The day such a principle is accepted, the true demise of the independence of the Judge in deciding cases before him is assured. The oath of the Judge is to do Justice according to law and to all manner of people, without fear or favour, affection or ill will."
Adolphus Godwin Karibi-Whyte, J.S.C.[19]

"...it is not the duty of the court to conduct cases for litigants; a court being likened to an umpire, should not jump into the arena to take part in the legal battle between parties.
Sylvester Umaru Onu, J.C.A.[20]

---

[17] Oghor v. State (1990) 3 NWLR (Pt.139) 484 at 501, H quoting Aniagolu, J.S.C. in Nwosu v. The State (1986) 4 NWLR (Pt.35) 348 at 359.
[18] Phoenix Motors Ltd v. N.P.F.M.B. (1993) 1 NWLR (Pt.272) 718 at 730, E-F
[19] Finnih v. Imade (1992) 1 NWLR (Pt.219) 511 at 537, E-F
[20] Nnodim v. Amadi (1993) 1 NWLR (Pt.271) 568 at 584, H

"Our system of law anticipates the Judge to manifest fairness all along, to hold an even balance. Once a Judge has decided that a claim cannot be maintained whereby he strikes it out or dismisses it, he is functus officio, and cannot reopen it by ordering an amendment. Should he hold that the action is not competent or cannot be maintained whereby he strikes out and dismisses it, that matter is no longer before him. To turn around and order amendment of what is no longer before him may unfortunately create the impression that he is no longer holding an even balance."
Salihu Modibbo Alfa Belgore, J.S.C.[21]

"If a Judge, said Lord Green, should himself conduct the examination of witnesses he, so to speak, descends into the arena and is liable to have his vision clouded by the dust of conflict. It is for the advocates, each in turn to examine the witnesses, and not for the Judge to take it on himself lest by so doing he appears to favour one side or the other."
Braimah Amen Omosun, J.C.A.[22]

"By the very nature of our adversary system, an adjudicator is expected to hold the balance between the parties evenly. He is not expected to move into the arena of the contest and participate in the proceedings to the advantage of one of the parties and disadvantage of the other party. That does not mean that an adjudicator cannot talk or intervene in the proceedings. He can, in deserving circumstances… An adjudicator is not a robot. Neither is he an imbecile. In order to be in a position to control the proceedings, he must be in a position to make

---

[21] Arubo v. Aiyeleru (1993) 3 NWLR (Pt.280) 126 at 147, C
[22] Nwankwo v. State (1990) 2 NWLR (Pt.134) 627 at 637, G quoting Lord Green in Yuill v. Yuill (1945) 1 All ER 185

interventions when necessary. That does not mean that he is taking sides or he is descending into the arena of the contest."
Niki Tobi, J.C.A.[23]

"... it is not the function of the Judge to discredit a witness called by one party by confronting him with his previous contrary evidence before another Judge. That role belongs to counsel for the opposing party. It is safe to say that a Judge's intervention must be governed by the bounden duty to see that a fair trial is enjoyed by the parties and that justice is not only done but seen to have been done."
Ephraim Omorose Ibukun Akpata, J.C.A.[24]

"... the justice which litigants expect in a court of law is even-handed justice reached in accordance with the law and the rules of the game. According to the basic principles of that form of justice, whoever must fail or succeed must do so without the assistance of the courts."
Philip Nnaemeka-Agu, J.S.C.[25]

"The hierarchy of the courts is established for a clear legal purpose. Parties are bound to follow the jurisdictional hierarchy of the courts. The law does not allow them to come to a court of their own choice and file legal process. That will be chaotic. The judicial system will be in disarray."
Niki Tobi, J.C.A.[26]

"The Nigerian Constitution is founded on the rule of law the primary meaning of which is that everything must be done

---

[23] Kurfi v. Mohammed (1993) 2 NWLR (Pt.277) 602 at 619, F-H
[24] Terytex (Nig) Ltd v. Nigerian Ports Authority (1989) 1 NWLR (Pt.96) 229 at 236, G
[25] Arubo v. Aiyeleru (1993) 3 NWLR (Pt.280) 126 at 143, D
[26] Ezegbu v. FATB Ltd (1992) 1 NWLR (Pt.216) 197 at 206, E-F

according to law. It means also that government should be conducted within the frame-work of recognized rules and principles which restrict discretionary power which Coke colourfully spoke of as 'golden and straight metwand of law as opposed to the uncertain and crooked cord of discretion' ..."

Andrews Otutu Obaseki, J.S.C.[27]

"The rule of natural justice has been with us from creation. Even God himself did not pass sentence upon Adam before he was called upon to enter on his defence. The Almighty God called upon Adam, have you eaten from the tree I warned you about? Genesis 3:1. The Lord gave him opportunity to defend himself before passing sentence upon him. Even the Romans, as it is borne out in the New Testament, Acts Chapter 25:16 during the trial of St. Paul upheld the maxim of *audi alteram partem* as follows: 'It is not the manner of the Romans to deliver any man to die, before that he which is accused have the accusers face to face, and has licence to answer for himself concerning the crime laid against him'."

Isa Ayo Salami, J.C.A.[28]

"A just fair and an organized society is that built upon a concept of natural justice, equity and good conscience. The said phenomenal principle is inbuilt and enshrined in the foundational framework existing and forming the basis of our Constitution."

Clara Bata Ogunbiyi, J.S.C.[29]

"The outcome of any criminal trial not only touches on the conscience of the society, it affects or controls its psyche.

---

[27] Governor of Lagos State v. Ojukwu (1986) 1 NWLR (Pt.18) 621 at 638, E-F
[28] Awuse v. Odili (2005) 16 NWLR (Pt.952) 515 at 529, E-H
[29] Awuse v. Odili (2005) 16 NWLR (Pt.952) 515 at 541, F-G

If it were not so the barbaric or kangaroo criminal justice system which applied or operated in the dark days of mankind would have still been prevalent till the present day. It was the sustained and concerted societal efforts that got the primitive and absolute backward system modified at every stage of human development until we got to the present evolution of our criminal justice system. The society is still not at rest in working out improvement of this system. Criminal justice system in a country that upholds the rule of law as a way of life cannot but conform with acceptable standard prevailing in all civilized countries of the world. I make bold to say that Nigeria is not an exception -we are in a democracy and the rule of law must prevail."

Pius Olayiwola Aderemi, J.C.A.[30]

"A law enforcement agent who is supposed to bring sanity and order on the road, brings out his gun and fire it just because a driver obstructs his right of passage…The mere fact that he deemed it necessary to bring out a gun is enough act of recklessness. I believe such rash acts must be stopped to prevent innocent human lives from being wasted."

Aloma Mariam Mukhtar, J.S.C.[31]

"The recourse to self-help measures by a party before seeking an assistance of the court is antithetical to the equitable relief of injunction. The law does not admit of self-help in mitigation of damage to reputation."

Kumai Bayang Akaahs, J.C.A.[32]

---

[30] Oladele v. Nigerian Army (2004) (Pt.868) 166 at 181, D-G
[31] Agbo v. State (2006) 6 NWLR (Pt.977) 545 at C-G
[32] Tell Communications Ltd v. Marwa (2006) 4 NWLR (Pt.970) 315 at 333, H

"In our democracy where the rule of law both in its conservative and contemporary constitutional meaning operates, the doors of the courts should be left wide open…This is a desideratum in our polity and the Constitution provides for it."
Niki Tobi, J.C.A.[33]

"Where the Rule of Law operates, the philosophy of self-help withdraws and law enforcement authorities of the State ensure that things are done according to law."
Andrews Otutu Obaseki, J.S.C.[34]

"The right to comment freely on matters of public interest is one of the fundamental rights of free speech guaranteed to the individual in our Constitution. It is so dear to the Nigerian and of vital importance and relevance to the rule of law which we so dearly treasure for our personal freedom."
Adolphus Godwin Karibi-Whyte, J.S.C.[35]

"The function of the court is to use the armoury of its rules to do justice in the matter. The armoury, for a change, cannot this time around, be weapons for war but for justice through peace and to the egalitarian advantage of the parties. Once rules become an affront and hurdle to or wedge against justice, the court is entitled to meander its way through the rules in search of justice. Once rules involve themselves in direct confrontation with justice, once rules directly antagonize the well settled principles of justice, the rules must invariably succumb and give way to justice par excellence."
Niki Tobi, J.C.A.[36]

---

[33] Reg. Trustees of Ifeloju v. Kuku (1991) 5 NWLR (Pt.189) 65 at 79, G-H
[34] Ukwunnenyi v. State (1989) 4 NWLR (Pt.114) 131 at 149, A
[35] Din v. African Newspapers Ltd (1990) 3 NWLR (Pt.139) 392 at 408-409, H-A
[36] Veritas Ins. Co. Ltd v. Citi Trust Inv. Ltd (1993) 3 NWLR (Pt.281) 349 at 369 F

"... the days when parties could pick their way in this court through naked technical rules of procedure the breach of which does not occasion a miscarriage of justice are fast sinking into the limbo of forgotten things. The courts now take the view that not every slip is fatal to the course of justice. Judges are not omniscient robots which never deviate from a programmed course."

Philip Nnaemeka-Agu, J.S.C.[37]

"While the doors of the court are open all through the day for litigants with genuine grievances to pursue their legitimate claims, the same doors will be shut against litigants who are merely busy bodies altercating or antagonizing the judicial process in precipitation, and for the fun of it. Certainly, the administration of justice will not encourage a plaintiff who has so much gluttony for litigation but who in real fact has no genuine complaint."

Niki Tobi, J.C.A.[38]

"Vengeance has no place in a society where the Rule of Law operates. The life of a person is more of an asset to the State and the State will not allow anyone to take the law into its own hands by avenging the death of a relation either on the culprit or on the innocent. The policy of avenging the death of a relation if allowed to take root will lead to a breakdown of law and order, to anarchy and eventually to the destruction of society itself."

Andrews Otutu Obaseki, J.S.C.[39]

---

[37] Nwosu v. Imo State Environmental Sanitation Authority (1990) 2 NWLR (Pt.135) 688 at 717, F-G
[38] Albion Construction Co. Ltd v. Rao Invest. & Properties Ltd (1992) 1 NWLR (Pt.219) 583 at 594, C-D
[39] Ukwunnenyi v. State (1989) 4 NWLR (Pt.114) 131 at 149, B

"Judicial precedent is an insurance against inconsistent judgments. In matters affecting the administration of justice, liberty of the subject, interests of justice, there cannot be a posture of indifference in the name of stare decisis so as to enthrone injustice. That in itself will amount to a negation of justice. Where there is cause to depart from previous decision this court will not hesitate to do so."

Olajide Olatawura, J.S.C.[40]

"The court is not entitled to stand on arid legalism by doing 'justice' to the rules and injustice to the matter before it. By that approach, the court has done 'justice' in inverted comas. The court has reversed justice and has done injustice. While a court of law should follow its rules, let it take the earliest opportunity to retrieve its steps when it is in the interest of justice to do so. It should not allow itself to fall headlong into a ditch in the course of following its rules. It can never remain afloat or alive to do justice. That will be serious. Litigants will not be happy. The courts themselves will not be happy too."

Niki Tobi, J.C.A.[41]

"A Judge exists to determine disputes and to examine with due care and microscopic sense all matters before him in his pursuit of justice. He is not there to trap any party or to set in motion what parties have not brought before him. He is not the Grand Inquisitor envisaged by Dostoevsky in his Brothers Karamazou. He is a Judge governed by rules."

George Adesola Oguntade, J.C.A.[42]

---

[40] Asanya v. State (1991) 3 NWLR (Pt.180) 422 at 475, H-A
[41] Veritas Ins. Co. Ltd v. Citi Trust Inv. Ltd (1993) 3 NWLR (Pt.281) 349 at 369, G
[42] Ndiwe v. Shinleton & Co. Ltd (1993) 2 NWLR (Pt.274) 242 at 250, C-D quoting Eso, J.S.C.in Sodipo v. Lemminkainen OY (No.1) (1986) 1 S.C. 197 at 217.

"It is not given to human justice to see and know, as the great Eternal knows, the thoughts and actions of all men. Human justice has to depend on evidence and inferences.... In our system, it is therefore better that nine guilty persons escape than that one innocent man is condemned. And that is why the court gives the benefit of any reasonable doubt to an accused person."
Chukwudifu Akunne Oputa, J.S.C.[43]

"It is of considerable interest that the administration of justice and the stability of our society and constitution that the thin and fragile fabric of our judicial wall should be protected from the wanton attacks of irate litigants whose only grievance is that they have lost their cause or falsely believe that they are persecuted. However, even where the grievance is right, where the effect is aimed at creating a destabilizing effect in the administration of justice, the greater interest of the public in the society and in the maintenance of an uninhibited administration of justice must prevail."
Adolphus Godwin Karibi-Whyte, J.S.C.[44]

"The law is the rule whereby the invisible border line is fixed within which the being and the activity of each individual obtains a secure and free space."
Ignatius Chukwudi Pats- Acholonu, J.C.A.[45]

"...in setting the yardstick of what amounts to unreasonable delay, a copy-cat adoption of what obtains elsewhere in the world would, in my mind, be to set up pitfalls into which society may end up badly hurt."
Sylvester Umaru Onu, J.S.C.[46]

---

[43] Ukwunnenyi v. State (1989) 4 NWLR (Pt.114) 131 at 156, D-E
[44] Egbe v. Adefarasin (1985) 1 NWLR (Pt.3) 549 at 567, G
[45] Houtmangracht v. Oduba (1995) 1 NWLR (Pt.371) 295 at 311 C, quoting Friedrich Von Savigny
[46] Effiom v. State (1995) 1 NWLR (Pt.373) 507 at 578, B

"I believe that in a young and developing democracy like ours, the court must understand certain factors that affect the society and adopt laws to social conditions and set up. It must be responsive to the needs of the time and be accommodating to be respectful not only in this country but in other countries as well."
Ignatius Chukwudi Pats-Acholonu, J.C.A.[47]

"...amid the clash of arms, the laws are not silent; they may be changed, but they speak the same language in war and in peace."
Francis Olisa Awogu, J.C.A.[48]

"Those that think that might is right and that the Government can do no wrong should better have a second thought. We have long passed that stage. Public servants who behave as if they are above the law, believing that their actions will be approved by the Government are not better than those deliberately set out on a collision course with the law."
Olajide Olatawura, J.S.C.[49]

"It is the public duty of everyone who knows or reasonably believes that a crime has been committed to assist in the discovery of the wrong-doer. Any complaint made, or information given, for that purpose to the Police, or to those interested in investigating the matter will, in the interest of society, be privileged and the mere fact that the information was volunteered will make no difference."
George Adesola Oguntade, J.C.A.[50]

---

[47] Houtmangracht v. Oduba (1995) 1 NWLR (Pt.371) 295 at 311, E-F
[48] NEC v. Nzeribe (1991) 5 NWLR (Pt.192) 458 at 470 F quoting Lord Atkins's dictum in Liversidge v. Anderson (1948), AC 206
[49] Osho v. Foreign Fin. Corp. (1991) 4 NWLR (Pt.184) 157 at 202, E-F
[50] Umagba v. Ogbe (1996) 8 NWLR (Pt.468) 621 at 626, E-F

"People who run or organise political parties recognised by the government should know that these parties are not close shops as they are democratic bodies founded to canvass for votes from the citizenry."

Ignatius Chukwudi Pats-Acholonu, J.C.A.[51]

"The law frowns at sophistry and it will be an affront to the administration of justice to exhibit a tendency that manifests a double-think on matters of principle."

Sule Aremu Olagunju, J.C.A.[52]

"The principle on which the defence of qualified privilege is founded is a universal one that the public convenience is to be preferred to private interests and that communication which the interest of society requires to be unfettered may freely be made by persons acting honestly without actual malice, notwithstanding that they involve relevant comments condemnatory of individuals."

Oludade Oladapo Obadina, J.C.A.[53]

"A person is entitled to his reputation and good name; if he is besmirched without good cause or justification, the defamed person is entitled to payment of damages."

Suleiman Galadima, J.C.A.[54]

"The laws of all civilized Nations have always frowned at self-help if for no other reason than that they engender breaches of peace."

Anthony Nnaemezie Aniagolu, J.S.C.[55]

---

[51] NTA v. Babatope (1996) 4 NWLR (Pt.440) 75 at 94, B-C
[52] Achebe v. Nwosu (2003) 7 NWLR (Pt.818) 103 at 135, H
[53] PGSS, Ikachi v. Igbudu (2005) 12 NWLR (Pt. 940) 543 at 574, F-G
[54] Ukachukwu v. Uzodinma (2007) 9 NWLR (Pt. 1938) 167 at 190-191, H-A
[55] Elochin (Nig.) Ltd v. Mbadiwe (1986) 1 NWLR (Pt.14) 47 at 60

"Whatever nomenclature or cognomen a Government Body or any other Body gives to itself or styles itself, (whether ministerial or administrative body) it is bound to follow the elementary rules of natural justice the moment its actions or inactions will affect the rights and interests of a person to his detriment. Not only the rules of natural justice demand that the position should be so. The Constitution of the land, the *fons et origo* of our legal system clearly demands such position."
Niki Tobi, J.C.A.[56]

"The desire of a court to do as many cases as possible is understandable; but in seeking to do that, it should not do so at the expense of giving a party a fair hearing."
Emmanuel Obioma Ogwuegbu, J.S.C.[57]

"A Judge, before he comes to a decision against a party, must hear and consider all that he has to say and the only fair way of reaching a correct decision on any dispute is for the Judge to hear all that is to be said on either side and then come to his conclusion. A hearing cannot be said to be fair if one of the parties is refused a hearing or not given an opportunity to be heard."
Emmanuel Obioma Ogwuegbu, J.S.C.[58]

"The corporate existence of Nigeria, it must be admitted; postulates the principle of co-operation between the three arms of government (Executive, Legislature and Judiciary). Where these work together in the same framework, then the rule of law shall prevail in that society. But where each selects to work in

---

[56] Steel Bell (Nig.) Ltd v. Govt. of Cross River State (1996) 3 NWLR (Pt.438) 571 at 589, H
[57] Olumesan v. Ogundepo (1996) 2 NWLR (Pt.433) 628 at 653, F
[58] Olumesan v. Ogundepo (1996) 2 NWLR (Pt. 433) 628 at 653, A

isolation and/or in utter disdain of the other, then havoc wrecks the society."

Ibrahim Tanko Muhammad, J.C.A.[59]

"If for any reason, the Executive arm of government refuses to comply with court orders, I am afraid that is promoting anarchy and executive indiscipline capable of wrecking the organic framework of the society."

Ibrahim Tanko Muhammad, J.C.A.[60]

"What was the situation in the simple old days? Nigeria did have laws before the advent of the British. It was certainly not a state of anarchy. The laws consisted of customs of the people, not codified - no means for such elegance - but written in the breast of the chiefs who were the undisputed leaders of the community..."

Moronkeji Omotayo Onalaja, J.C.A.[61]

"I am of the firm view that for a nation such as ours, to have stability and respect for democracy, obviously rule of law must be allowed to follow its normal course unencumbered."

Ibrahim Tanko Muhammad, J.C.A.[62]

"...it is indeed a sorry situation that ...highly placed government functionaries should descend so low to disobey a clear order of this court with reckless abandon. They are supposed to set good example for the people to follow, but instead they tenaciously promoted indiscipline of the highest order by openly promoting lawlessness in our nation from the vantage point of their seat of

---

[59] Ibrahim v. Emein (1996) 2 NWLR (Pt.430) 322 at 337, C
[60] Ibrahim v. Emein (1996) 2 NWLR (Pt.430) 322 at 337, B
[61] Whyte v. Jack (1996) 2 NWLR (Pt.431) 407 at 449, B-C quoting from the book of Kayode Eso, J.S.C.- "Nigerian Grundnorm" at page 39
[62] Ibrahim v. Emein (1996) 2 NWLR (Pt.430) 322 at 337, B

power. It is indeed very regrettable to place such type of people in a position of authority."

Umaru Abdullahi, J.C.A.[63]

"I feel justified in saying that in the administration of justice, no Judge is permitted to resort to whims which turn out to be viewed as impeding the course of justice."

Samson Odemwingie Uwaifo, J.C.A.[64]

"Any legally qualified person holding the esteemed office of the Attorney-General cannot allow himself to be sycophantic. His own responsibility is to offer his candid advice according to how he understands the issue involved uninfluenced by any consideration... And I think it is more honourable always in a situation where you cannot beat them, then you better bulge out instead of following them."

Ibrahim Tanko Muhammad, J.C.A.[65]

"Nigeria is a democracy and by the grace of the Almighty God it will remain a democracy for all times. The foundation of any democracy is anchored on the Rule of Law both in its conservative and contemporary meaning... Once we fail to uphold the Rule of Law, anarchy, despotism and totalitarianism will pervade the entire society. The social equilibrium will be broken. Law and order breaks down. Everybody will be his own keeper and God for us all. We, as Judges, cannot afford to see society decay to such an irreparable level. We must rise up fully

---

[63] Ibrahim v. Emein (1996) 2 NWLR (Pt.430) 322 at 333, F-G
[64] TSA Ind. Ltd v. Abacus Merchant Bank Ltd (1996) 2 NWLR (Pt.430) 305 at 317, D
[65] Ibrahim v. Emein (1996) 2 NWLR (Pt.430) 322 at 337, G-H

to our duties by vindicating the tenets of the Rule of Law in our practiced democracy."

Niki Tobi, J.C.A.[66]

"It is antithetical to the idea and practice of the rule of law for anyone to render the judiciary ineffective through any subterfuge, or by sheer exercise of absolute authority or by in terrorem posturing. It is even so when a glittering façade of judicial independence is presented upon some identified grundnorm only to seek to protect every governmental action by ouster clause."

Samson Odemwingie Uwaifo, J.S.C.[67]

"The rule of law knows no fear. It is never cowed down; it can only be silenced by the only arm that can silence it, it must be accepted in full confidence to be able to justify its existence."

Kayode Eso, J.S.C.[68]

"In the realm of criminal proceedings, I find particularly apposite the opinion of Irikefe, J.S.C. as he then was in Echeazu v. Commissioner of Police (1974) 2 SC 55 at 69-70 that while certain provisions of our law affords an accused person adequate safeguards, it is clearly not the intention of the makers of these rules that they should provide such an accused with a gratuitous "escape route" to freedom in the face of overwhelming evidence."

Sule Aremu Olagunju, J.C.A.[69]

---

[66] Onagoruwa v. IGP (1991) 5 NWLR (Pt.193) 593 at 650 C-D
[67] A-G Federation v. Guardian Newspaper Ltd (1999) 9 NWLR (Pt.618) 187 at 214, F-G
[68] Garba v. Federal Civil Service Commission (1988) 19 NSCC (Pt.1) 306 at 320
[69] Uwagba v. Federal Republic of Nigeria (2000) 13 NWLR (Pt.684) at 251, C (referring to the opinion of Irikefe, J.S.C. in Echeazu v. Commissioner of Police (1974) 2 SC 55 at 69-70

"There seems to be no legal warrant or judicial discretion for prying into the observance of unwritten procedural rules fashioned for convenience. Such in my opinion are non-justiciable, and if for anything should be avoided for their uncertainty."

Adolphus Godwin Karibi-Whyte, J.S.C.[70]

"…it is not the law that once an ouster of jurisdiction clause is raised in any proceeding, the court must automatically throw in the towel, decline jurisdiction and proceed to strike out the suit… but has a duty to inquire into the issue to enable it to determine whether or not it has jurisdiction."

Sylvester Umaru Onu, J.S.C.[71]

"Freedom is no doubt the greatest gift or heritage of man. Omnipotence created man and accorded him with divine freedom. Men are born free with liberty to think what he will… without let or hindrance from any other persons, private or government authorities. I am not oblivious of the fact that there are checks and balances to the series of freedom given."

Pius Olayiwola Aderemi, J.C.A.[72]

"…judicial discretion is a term applied to the discretionary action of a Judge or court and means discretion bounded by the rules and principles of law, and not arbitrary, capricious, or unrestrained. It is not the indulgence of judicial whim, but the exercise of judicial judgment, based on facts and guided by law, or the equitable of what is just and proper under the circumstances. It is a legal discretion to be exercised in

---

[70] A.-G., Federation v. Guardian Newspaper Ltd (1999) 9 NWLR (Pt.618) 187 at 239, E
[71] A.-G., Federation v. Guardian Newspaper Ltd (1999) 9 NWLR (Pt.618) 187 at 255, F
[72] Comptroller of Nigeria Prisons v. Adekanye (1999) 10 NWLR (Pt.623) 400 at 421, G-H

discerning the course prescribed by law and is not to give effect to the will of the Judge, but to that of the law."

Ibrahim Tanko Muhammad, J.C.A.[73]

"The functions of the Attorney General always touch on the conscience of the society. To move the court to prevent him from performing his duties is to do greater harm to the psyche of the society."

Pius Olayiwola Aderemi, J.C.A.[74]

"If a community which is not constituted into a Court of Law imposes a fine, it is illegal and this court will not lend a helping hand to illegality under the pretext of well-being of a Community."

Atinuke Ige, J.C.A.[75]

"Justice would lose its ethical or moral meaning, and sink to a mere charitable treatment of the enslaved and the oppressed by those in power, without the involvement of the people in designing their legal system. The law-giver will continue to stand above the law which he manipulates to entrench himself and fortify his position. He will not be concerned with justice and legality, in their true sense except to use these as slogans for keeping faith with the people."

Ignatius Chukwudi Pats-Acholonu, J.C.A.[76]

"...I should here say that it is much to be desired that newspapers, television or news media generally should be free to bring to

---

[73] Folorunsho v. Folorunsho (1996) 5 NWLR (Pt. 450) 612 at 620, G-H
[74] Bagudu v. FRN (2004) 1 NWLR (Pt. 853) 182 at 206, E-F
[75] Ojuya v. Nzeogwu (1996) 1 NWLR (Pt. 427) 713 at 724, C
[76] Guardian Newspaper Ltd v. A.G. Federation (1995) 5 NWLR (Pt. 398) 703 at 738, F-G quoting Professor Ogwurike in his book titled "Concept of Law in English Speaking Africa" at page 194

the notice of the public any matter of public interest or concern. But in order to be deserving of that freedom, the press must show itself worthy of it. A free press cannot be deserving of that appellation unless it is a responsible press. The power of the press is enormous. It must not abuse that power… The press, in a society that upholds the law as a way of life, has a seldom duty to feed the society with true facts and honest comments. That crucial function, in my view, tantamounts to moulding positively public opinion."

Pius Olayiwola Aderemi, J.C.A.[77]

"In the scheme of things and the governance of the country, the Attorney-General occupies a very special position. He is duty bound to protect the citizens of the country against arbitrary executive acts. By virtue of his training and calling, the Attorney-General acts as the link man between the citizens and all organs of the government. In my view, his duty to prosecute palpable criminal matters is not higher than his duty to protect citizens from executive lawlessness."

Dahiru Musdapher, J.C.A.[78]

"I have deemed it compelling to reiterate the trite axiom, that a blatant disrespect to a court of law, in whatever ramification is antithetical to the rule of law; the fundamental objectives of democracy, and the well cherished independence of the judiciary."

Helen Moronkeji Ogunwumiju, J.C.A[79]

---

[77] Gomes v. Punch (Nig.) Ltd (1999) 5 NWLR (Pt.602) 303 at 311 - 312
[78] A-G. Federation v. Ajayi (1996) 5 NWLR (Pt.448) 283 at 290 paras. B-C
[79] Zenith Bank v George C. Igbokwe & Anor. (2013) LPELR 21975 (pp.27-28para F-D) (CA)

"If a court is already seised of a matter it behoves the government to allow the law to take its course or to allow the legal and judicial process to run its full course."

> Ignatius Chukwudi Pats-Acholonu, J.C.A.[80]

"Those who won our independence believe that the final end of the state was to make men free to develop their faculties and that in its government the deliberate forces should prevail over the arbitrary... Recognising the occasional tyrannies of government majorities, they amended the Constitution so that free speech should be guaranteed."

> Ignatius Chukwudi Pats-Acholonu, J.C.A.[81]

"...where commitment to rule of law is a policy of State and has always been an operative ideal of society as in this country, it cannot be the intention of the law maker that abuse of power and arbitrariness should be sanctioned or go uncorrected."

> Emmanuel Olayinka Ayoola, J.C.A.[82]

"Law in Africa must be conceived of and evaluated in terms of its social purpose, function and the value system, the spirit of the time, the tempo of socio-economic and political development in the new States, and above all, the greatest happiness of the masses should be the main guiding principles underlying legal development."

> Ignatius Chukwudi Pats-Acholonu, J.C.A.[83]

---

[80] N.I.O. & M. R. v. Okonya (1996) 4 NWLR (Pt.444) 611 at620 paras. F-G
[81] Guardian Newspaper Ltd. v. A.G. Federation (1995) 5 NWLR (Pt.398) 703 at 737-738, H-D quoting Mr. Justice Brandels in Whitney v. California 274 US 367 89 Guardian Newspaper Ltd v. A.-G., Federation (1995) 5 NWLR (Pt. 398) 703 at 752, C
[82] Guardian Newspaper Ltd v. A.-G., Federation (1995) 5 NWLR (Pt.398) 703 at 752, C
[83] Guardian Newspaper Ltd v. A.-G., Federation (1995) 5 NWLR (Pt.398) 703 at 738, H quoting Professor Ogwurike in his book titled "Concept of Law in English Speaking Africa" at page 194

"If the rule of law is to be maintained, the court must use its jurisdiction to prevent disobedience to laws, which exercise of powers without regard to the empowering statute entails, and, to prevent arbitrariness which immunity from accountability for administrative actions which affect right of others promotes."
Emmanuel Olayinka Ayoola, J.C.A.[84]

"It must be emphasised that no party before a court should do anything to undermine the authority of the court. When that is done, it is a challenge to the administration of justice and in an appropriate case will be visited with the proper sanction."
Samson Odemwingie Uwaifo, J.C.A.[85]

"I think that the express statutory provision for remand or detention of a person puts it beyond conjecture that the detention is constitutionally protected and clothed with the toga of legality which ought not to be questioned."
Okay Achike, J.C.A.[86]

"...true justice particularly where allegations of untoward acts have been made against someone, to be premised on right reason, must be in accord with dictates of fair play and natural justice."
Ignatius Chukwudi Pats-Acholonu, J.C.A.[87]

"...where the police or the executive arbitrarily detain a citizen in the circumstances outside the purview of... law, then that is derogatory to due process of law and antithetical to democracy.

---

[84] Guardian Newspaper Ltd v. A.G. Federation (1995) 5 NWLR (Pt.398) 703 at 753, C-D
[85] Hallmark Bank Ltd v. Akaluso (1995) 5 NWLR (Pt.395) 306 at 313, G
[86] Chinemelu v. C.O.P. (1995) 4 NWLR (Pt.390) 467 at 483, D
[87] Ozoana v. P.S.C. (1995) 4 NWLR (Pt.391) 629 at 639, A-B

That will signal a head-on romance with anarchy and a police State."

Okay Achike, J.C.A.[88]

"Judges and courts exercise their discretion in accordance with rule of law and justice and not according to private opinion. An exercise of discretion is a liberty or privilege to decide and act in accordance with what is fair and equitable under the peculiar circumstances of the particular case, guided by the spirit and principles of law."

Idris Legbo Kutigi, J.S.C.[89]

"The Constitution is the supreme law of the land. It is superior to any other statutes. It is the barometer on which the constitutionality or otherwise of a statute is measured."

Olufunlola Oyelola Adekeye, J.C.A.[90]

"The fundamental rights have not been put in the Constitution merely for individual benefit, though ultimately they come into operation in considering individual rights. They have been put there as a matter of public policy and the doctrine of waiver can have no application to provisions of law which have been enacted as a matter of constitutional policy."

Philip Nnaemeka-Agu, J.S.C.[91]

"The Constitution is the life wire of any legal system. It is the first point of reference as well as the terminal point of reference in term of determining the legal strength of any statute. Being the life wire of the legal system, the jurisdiction conferred on

---

[88] Chinemelu v. C.O.P. (1995) 4 NWLR (Pt.390) 467 at 483, E
[89] M.V. Lupex v. N.O.C. & S. Ltd. (2003) 15 NWLR (Pt.844) at 488, paras F-G
[90] Abacha v. FRN (2006) 4 NWLR (Pt.970) 239 at 311, B-C
[91] Enigwe v. Akaigwe (1992) 2 NWLR (Pt.225) 505 at 536B (quoting former Chief Justice of India in Behram Khurshid Pesikaka v. Bombay State (1955) AIR 42 at 123

the courts by the Constitution cannot ordinarily be thrown overboard without doing any violence."

Niki Tobi, J.C.A.[92]

"A constitution must always be construed in such a way that it protects what it sets to protect or guides what it sets out to guide. By its very nature and by necessity, a constitution must be interpreted broadly in order not to defeat the clear intention of its framers."

Dennis Onyejife Edozie, J.C.A.[93]

"When the courts and the executive recognize the limits of their power under the Constitution and reciprocally respect and regard each other, the result to society is a harmonious relationship which fosters stability in society and glaringly exposes the concept of the Rule of Law. This is what is universally acknowledged as Constitutional Governance…. It is the readiness of the executive to accept even unfavourable judgments gracefully; that is the hallmark and signpost for characterizing a Government as responsible and conducting its affairs in accordance with the Rule of Law. Judges go and Judges come but the Rule of Law should remain."

George Adesola Oguntade, J.C.A.[94]

"If government treats court order with levity and contempt, the confidence of the citizen in the court will be seriously eroded and the effect of that will be the beginning of anarchy in replacement of the rule of law. If anyone should be wary of orders of court it is the authorities; for they, more than anyone

---

[92] Adeniyi v. Oroja (1992) 4 NWLR (Pt.235) 322 at 343, E
[93] Adamu v. A.G. Borno State (1996) 8 NWLR (Pt.465) 203 at 223, H
[94] Doma v. Ogiri (1998) 3 NWLR (Pt.541) 246 at 269, B-D

else, need the application of the rule of law in order to govern properly and effectively."

Muhammadu Lawal Uwais, J.S.C.[95]

"Civil Servants are no robots. They are, or should be interested in the running of the affairs of the government. They are paid to work and to point out, where necessary, wrongs by public officials or members of the public. ... Another legitimate duty is to correct the ills of the public. They should not by so doing be punished and regarded as obstructionists. ... The nation needs men and women of probity in all sectors of the public service."

Olajide Olatawura, J.S.C.[96]

"The function of the Constitution is to establish a framework and principles of government, broad and general in terms intended to apply to the varying conditions which the development of our several communities must involve, ours being a plural, dynamic society..."

Udo Udoma, J.S.C.[97]

"Without a strict adherence to the rule of law, our nascent democracy and, indeed, our Constitution will only be worth the paper on which it is written. What makes a great country is adherence to the rule of law. Even in hell, there is order and discipline."

Sotonye Denton-West, J.C.A.[98]

"A claim, in a court, in present day Nigeria, with slavery as foundation, or even a remote, linkage is mildly put, aberrant...

---
[95] Military Governor of Lagos State v. Ojukwu (1986) 2 SC 277 at 298-299
[96] Bakare v. Lagos State Civil Service Commission (1992) 8 NWLR (Pt.262) 641 at 705, B-C
[97] Nafiu Rabiu v. The State (1981) 2 NCLR 293 at 326.
[98] Balonwu v. Obi (2007) 5 NWLR (Pt.1028) 488 at 563, B

From historical facts and testimonies, all the members of the human race are like rational creatures originating from one Heavenly beneficent Creator and in all respects, equally endowed by Him. Slave-drivers, if any exists today, should be profoundly apologetic rather than assert any imagined right"
Monica B. Dogban-Mensem, J.C.A.[99]

"It is up to the police to protect our nascent democracy and not the military; otherwise, the democracy might be wittingly or unwittingly militarized. This is not what the citizenry bargained for after power from the military in 1999. Conscious step or steps should be taken to civilianize the polity and thereby ensure survival and sustenance of democracy"
Isa Ayo Salami, J.C.A.[100]

"A court should never allow a fundamental provision of the Constitution guaranteeing parties the right to fair trial within a reasonable time in resolution of their dispute, be held hostage by either laziness or deliberate tardiness of counsel. The court owes a sacred duty to protect and ensure compliance with that constitutional guarantee and not to give the impression of non-challance..."
Mohammed Lawal Garba, J.C.A.[101]

"A good leader should adhere to law and observe same. Leaders cannot exist without followership and so everyone must observe the Constitution and obey State authorities, because no authority exists without God's permission, and the existing authorities

---

[99] Nwosu v. Uche (2005) 17 NWLR (Pt.955) 574 at 595 C, F-G
[100] Yusuf v. Obasanjo (2005) 18 NWLR (Pt.956) 96 at C-D
[101] Alabi v. Doherty (2005) 18 NWLR (Pt.957) 411 at 437, E-F

have been put in place by God who had allowed them to swear to an oath to uphold the Constitution."
Sotonye Denton-West, J.C.A.[102]

"I however make bold to remind the authorities that the Constitution presumes that everyone charged with an offence is presumed innocent until proven guilty. The practice of keeping suspects in deplorable conditions while in custody pending their trial is a glaring misinterpretation of the Constitution. It is akin to running a modern age Gestapo - a concentration camp"
Olufunlola Oyelola Adekeye, J.C.A.[103]

"Welfare of child is not the material provisions in the house -good clothes, food, air conditioners, television, all the gadgets normally associated with the middle class, - it is more of happiness of the child and his psychological development. While it is good a child is brought up by complementary care of the two parents living happily together, it is psychologically detrimental to his welfare and ultimate happiness and psychological development if material care, available, is denied him."
Salihu Modibbo Alfa Belfore, J.S.C.[104]

"It is the duty of the Government to endeavour to equip both the police and prisons departments so that they could not be found wanting in the performance of their duties. However, taking shelter under those inadequacies in order to claim breach of a constitutional right is unfair and unjust."
Uthman Mohammed, J.S.C.[105]

---

[102] Ibid at 562, B-C
[103] Fasehun v. A.-G., Federation (2006) 6 NWLR (Pt.975) 141 at 153-154, H-A
[104] Odogwu v. Odogwu (1992) 2 NWLR (Pt.225) 539 at 559, H-A
[105] Effiom v. State (1995) 1 NWLR (Pt.373) 507 at 519, E-F

"The existence of Nigeria as a nation is a product of law, the Constitution, and this makes the legal profession a unique body whose internal discipline must not be taken for granted."
                    Salihu Modibbo Alfa Belgore, J.S.C.[106]

"The purport of fair hearing is not to allow an unserious counsel to perpetually frustrate justice by holding the court to ransom; rather, the purport of fair hearing is the interest of justice and justice delayed is justice denied."
                    Sotonye Denton-West, J.C.A.[107]

"Fair hearing demands that all parties to a suit be given adequate opportunity to be heard on any matter in dispute between them. It is a fundamental concept which is enshrined in the Constitution"
                    Gertrude Ifunanya Udom-Azogu, J.C.A.[108]

"Fair hearing within the meaning of section 36 (1) of the 1999 Constitution of the Federal Republic of Nigeria means trial or investigation conducted according to all rules formulated to ensure justice is done to the parties. In its essence, fair hearing is not a technical doctrine but a doctrine of substance based on facts."
                    Chidi Nwaoma Uwa, J.C.A.[109]

"Fair hearing judicially defined does not admit the invocation of equitable powers of the court to deny persons rights so jealously guarded and guaranteed."
                    Musa Dattijo Muhammad, J.C.A.[110]

---

[106] Okike v. LPDC (2005) 15 NWLR (Pt.949) 471 at 518-519, H-A
[107] Agbabiaka v. FBN Plc (2007) 6 NWLR (Pt.1029) 25 at 44, F
[108] Amanchukwu v. FRN (2007) 6 NWLR (Pt.1029) 1 at 19, D
[109] PDP v. Abubakar (2007) 3 NWLR (Pt.1022) 515 at 547, D-F
[110] Guinness (Nig.) Ltd v. Udeani (2000) 14 NWLR (Pt.687) 367 at 391, G-C

"Fair hearing means a trial conducted according to all legal rules formulated to ensure that justice is done to all parties. Reasonable time must mean the period of time which, in the search for justice, does not wear out the parties..."

Andrews Otutu Obaseki, J.S.C.[111]

"The principles of natural justice enshrined in the *audi alteram partem* and *nemo debet esse judex in propria causa* are fundamental to the Nigerian system of adjudication and once they are breached, the trial or proceeding loses its credibility or validity however sound or rational the reasoning of the court might be."

Isa Ayo Salami, J.C.A.[112]

"...fair hearing in a properly constituted court or tribunal is an essential pre-requisite to peace and stability in society. The only alternative to it is chaos and jungle justice. Every member of the Nigerian society is as much interested in the peace and stability of the nation as the litigant in court who must have qualitative justice for him to be satisfied, win or lose."

Philip Nnaemeka-Agu, J.S.C.[113]

"Fair hearing... as a matter of law is the pivot upon which the entire judicial process or the administration of justice revolves. It is the keystone of the trial process as no trial can be sustained unless it accords with the principle of fair hearing..."

Niki Tobi, J.C.A.[114]

---

[111] Ariori v. Muraino (1983) 1 SC 13 at 24
[112] N.A.A. v. Orjiakor (1998) 6 NWLR (Pt.553) 265 at 277-278, A-H
[113] Enigwe v. Akaigwe (1992) 2 NWLR (Pt.225) 505 at 535-536, H-A
[114] Emerah v. Chiekwe (1996) 7 NWLR (Pt. 462) 536 at 548, A-B

"It is fundamental in that the Judge be all through seen as an impartial umpire who does not descend into the arena of the battle lest his vision might be obscured by the smoke emanating from the conflict.
Philip Nnaemeka-Agu, J.S.C.[115]

"The 'independence' and 'impartiality' of a court are part of the attributes of fair hearing."
Raphael Olufemi Rowland, J.C.A.[116]

"Care should be taken by the Court always not to sacrifice justice on the altar of technicalities. The time is no more when disputes are dealt with rather on technicalities and not on merit."
Kayode Eso, J.S.C.[117]

"The right of a party to be heard is important but must be confined within the circumscribed limits. It is never allowed to run wild."
Suleiman Galadima, J.C.A.[118]

"Fair hearing is not a cut and dry principle which the parties can, in the abstract, always apply to their comfort and convenience for, it is a principle which is based on facts of the case before the court."
Sotonye Denton-West, J.C.A.[119]

"Fair hearing is a concept of justice which should not be viewed from the perspective or prism of only one party."
Isa Ayo Salami, J.C.A.[120]

---

[115] Enigwe v. Akaigwe (1992) 2 NWLR (Pt.225) 505 at 531, para H
[116] Chevron (Nig.) Ltd v. Onwugbelu (1996) 3 NWLR (Pt.437) 404 at 417, G
[117] Chinwendu v. Mbamali (1980) 3 to 4 SC 31 at 80-81
[118] Ajidahun v. Ajidahun (2000) 4 NWLR (Pt.654) 605 at 615, E
[119] Apatira v. Lagos Island Local Govt. Council & Ors (2006) 17 (Pt.1007) 46 at 62, E-F
[120] Ayalogu v. Agu (1998) 1 NWLR (Pt.532) 129 at 144, E

"Where a party to a suit has been accorded a reasonable opportunity of being heard and in the manner prescribed under the law, and for no satisfactory explanation it fails or neglects to do that which he ought to do, the party cannot thereafter be heard to complain of lack of fair hearing."
Okay Achike, J.C.A.[121]

"Leaving facts until the last minute in the journey of a case to emerge will definitely put the other side at a disadvantage, and thus result in a miscarriage of justice. If, on the other hand, the opponent is given the opportunity to do justice to the amendments sought, it will be like starting the case all over again, and thus result in a senseless waste of time and energy."
Aloma Mariam Mukhtar, J.S.C.[122]

"It is a breach of the rule of natural justice of fair hearing to deny the opponent to an action in court, the right to be heard before penalty is imposed on him. It is also a breach of our Constitution."
Victor Aimepomo Oyeleye Omage, J.C.A.[123]

"Fair hearing does not contemplate a standard of justice which is biased in favour of one party and to the prejudice of the other. ...the bulk for raising the issue of fair hearing stops with being given the opportunity to be heard in the trial of a case within the scope so allowed by the pertinent law and rules of court."
Christopher Mitchell Chukwuma-Eneh, J.C.A.[124]

---

[121] Kaduna Textiles Ltd v. Umar (1994) 1 NWLR (Pt.319) 143 at 159, G
[122] Salako v. Williams (1998) 11 NWLR (Pt.547) 505 at 520, D-E
[123] Afric Mining Co. Ltd v. N.I.D.B. Ltd (2000) 2 NWLR (Pt.646) 618 at 629, A-B
[124] Ansa v. Cross Lines Ltd (2005) 14 NWLR (Pt. 946) 645 at 668, E-F

"The right to fair hearing is not an expression of mere rhetoric or empty verbalism, but a fundamental right of the individual guaranteed in the Constitution, the breach of which will nullify the proceedings in favour of the victim."

Niki Tobi, J.S.C.[125]

"The test of fair hearing as settled by all judicial authorities on the issue, is objective and the opinion of a reasonable person formed from his observation of the proceedings, if justice was done."

Mohammed Lawal Garba, J.C.A.[126]

"Bias removes the concept of justice and fair hearing; thus, contravening our very constitutional safeguard by eroding its foundational purport."

Clara Bata Ogunbiyi, J.S.C.[127]

"A right to fair hearing free from bias or likelihood of bias is a fundamental constitutional right and its breach in any trial nullifies the trial."

Dahiru Musdapher, J.C.A.[128]

"…it will leave a sorry memory of an emasculated judiciary to be persuaded by the argument that because of the sanctity of the constitutional right of fair hearing guaranteed to the citizenry encompassing the right of appeal an accused person who went underground to evade a judicial trial should be allowed while

---

[125] Gbadamosi v. Dairo (2007) 3 NWLR (Pt.1021) 282 at 306, A-B
[126] Zaboley Inter'l Ltd v. Omogbehin (2005) 17 NWLR (Pt.953) 200 at 223, G
[127] Yakubu v. State (2007) 9 NWLR (Pt.1038) 1 at 19, E-F
[128] Alake v. Abalaka (2003) 6 NWLR (Pt.815) 124 at 143

operating from the hideout to use the appellate outfit of the same judicial system to challenge the decision of the trial court that is adverse to him. That will be preposterous."
Sule Aremu Olagunju, J.C.A.[129]

"Fair hearing is not a one-way affair. It affects both parties."
Stanley Shenko Alagoa, J.C.A.[130]

"Fair hearing does not permit a litigant to hold a court to ransom or permit for a delay of justice."
Ibrahim Tanko Muhammad, J.C.A.[131]

"It is well established that the right to fair hearing cannot be waived or its breach acquiesced in fair hearing entails giving somebody an opportunity to explain his actions."
Theresa Ngolika Orji Abadua, J.C.A.[132]

"It is further stated that at the proceeding where principle of fair hearing are observed there is invariably atmosphere of calm in which witnesses can deliver their testimony without fear and intimidation, in which counsel can assert the accused's rights, freely and in which the truth may be received and given credence without fear of violence."
Theresa Ngolika Orji- Abadua, J.C.A.[133]

"A free and voluntary confession by a person if direct and positive, duly made and satisfactorily proved has been described

---

[129] Uwagba v. Fed. Republic of Nigeria (2000) 13 NWLR (Pt.684) at 251, E
[130] Darma v. Oceanic Bank Int'l (Nig.) Ltd (2005) 4 NWLR (Pt.915) 391 at 408, E
[131] Rabiu v. State (2005) 7 NWLR (Pt.925) 491 at 507, G
[132] Muhammed v. A.B.U., Zaria (2014) 7 NWLR (Pt.1407) at 531, para. B
[133] Muhammed v. A.B.U., Zaria (2014) 7 NWLR (Pt.1407) at 531, paras. D-E

as occupying: '.... the highest place of authenticity when it comes to proving beyond reasonable doubt."

Onyekachi Aja Otisi, J.C.A.[134]

"In the realm of law, sentiments or sympathy have no place. It is only law and law only that should take its course."

Ibrahim Tanko Muhammad, J.S.C.[135]

---

[134] Effiong v. State (2017) 2 NWLR (Pt.1549) 205 at 230, paras. F-G
[135] Okpe v. Fan Milk Plc. (2017) 2 NWLR (Pt. 1549) 282 at 310, B-C

2 DUTY OF COUNSEL TO THE COURT AND SOCIETY

"In a free society (which we claim to belong), it is the duty of lawyers to show enviable leadership by the way they conduct their cases with courage and elegance. They must realize that being officers in the temple of justice, it behoves of them to seek the supreme welfare of promotion of justice, the growth of jurisprudence and by their counseling and advocacy, they help to mould the public opinion as to what justice is."
Ignatius Chukwudi Pats-Acholonu, J.C.A.[136]

"Counsel owe the court an equal responsibility to ensure that they employ their best skill to see that they do not clog the wheel of the administration of justice."
Owolabi Kolawole, J.C.A.[137]

"Sentiments command no place in judicial deliberations for if it did, our task would be infinitely more difficult and less beneficial to the society."
Andrews Otutu Obaseki, J.S.C.[138]

"It is unethical and an affront to public policy to pass on the burden of Solicitor's fees to the other party."
Saka Adeyemi Ibiyeye, J.C.A.[139]

"Learned counsel on appeal should not behave like a drowning man clinging to any straw by filing frivolous, unmeritorious, and complaint amounting to gross abuse of the process of court."
Moronkeji Omotayo Onalaja, J.C.A.[140]

---

[136] Kotoye v. Saraki (1995) 6 NWLR (Pt.402) 504 at 508, G-H
[137] Anibire v. Womiloju (1993) 5 NWLR (Pt.295) 623 at 636, D
[138] Ezeugo v. Ohanyere (1978) 6-7 SC 171 at 184, para.30
[139] Guinness Nig. Plc v. Nwoke (2000) 15 NWLR (Pt.689) 135 at 150, C
[140] Aseimo v. Abraham (1994) 8 NWLR (Pt.361) 191 at 222, F

"Visiting the sin of counsel on his client is not permitted by law courts. …what is not however, tolerated is where a counsel committed blunder which must affect his case, such as filing a wrong or an incompetent process (such as originating process), there is no way the court can blind its eyes to allow the process have its way as such."

Ibrahim Tanko Muhammad, J.S.C.[141]

"For it is commonly believed by any discerning member of the public and of course the government that the deepest convictions of most citizens are that for meaningful progress of people to be of any use, the legal profession - nay the bar must be strong, virile and respected by all."

Ignatius Chukwudi Pats-Acholonu, J.C.A.[142]

"…Counsel owe it a duty to the courts to help reduce the period of delay in determining cases in courts by avoiding unnecessary preliminary objections so that the adage "justice delayed is justice denied" may cease to apply to the proceedings in court."

Olufunlola Oyelola Adekeye, J.C.A.[143]

"Counsel owes a duty to his client and the court to make accurate and specific references to a document he relies upon in vindication of the case of his client. He has to be exact and precise. In a case where the documentation is enormous, counsel will be helpful to the court to clearly and specifically found upon the document he is relying upon. Where this is not done, the court will be left to float in an ocean and it can never come

---

[141] Okpe v. Fan Milk Plc. (2017) 2 NWLR (Pt.1549) 282 at 310-311, H-A
[142] Williams v. Akintunde (1995) 3 NWLR (Pt.381) 101 at 114, G
[143] First Fuels Ltd v. NNPC (2007) 2 NWLR (Pt.1018) 276 at 301, C-D

ashore with the document. That will be bad, not for the court, but for the client."

Niki Tobi, J.C.A.[144]

"...counsel qua advocate is professionally knowledgeable in law and that is why he is briefed by his client. The facts of the case are not his. The facts of the case belong exclusively to his client and he has no business to flirt with them. His only duty is to make use of the facts presented to him by his client in the light of the law to persuade the court to give judgment to his client by employing his professional ability of persuasive advocacy. No more and no less."

Niki Tobi, J.C.A.[145]

"It is now time to warn that an advocate must stock his library with up-to-date law reports. An advocate is either in the practice of the profession or he sits content with the duties of a Solicitor in chambers."

Owolabi Kolawole, J.C.A.[146]

"The Supreme Court and this Court have said time without number that counsel should avoid the temptation of advocating the merits of a matter at the interlocutory stage. They should keep their gun powder dry and shoot at the appropriate time, and the appropriate time is when the merits of the matter are heard."

Niki Tobi, J.C.A.[147]

---

[144] Veritas Ins. Co. Ltd v. Citi Trust Inv. Ltd (1993) 3 NWLR (Pt.281) 349 at 367-368, H-A
[145] Albion Construction Co. Ltd v. Rao Invest. & Properties Ltd (1992) 1 NWLR (Pt.219) 583 at 596, F-G
[146] Nwokoro v. Nwosu (1990) 1 NWLR (Pt.129) 679 at 684, E
[147] Cocoa Merchant Ltd v. Commodities Sales Ltd (1993) 1 NWLR (Pt.271) 627 at 637, D

"The authority or right of the leading counsel in a case to address the court where there are junior counsels is a rule of practice which has the force of law. If, however the leading counsel announces that one of his junior counsel will address the court or conduct the case, the senior is equally bound by the result of the case. To shift responsibility thereafter is to engage in a game of hide and seek...The question of fair hearing does not arise..."

Olajide Olatawura, J.S.C.[148]

"The law is commonplace that counsel cannot dabble with the facts of the case as presented by his client. He is not allowed by the law to tell a different story from that told by his client. After all, the facts belong exclusively to his client. All he has is the law. That is his expertise."

Niki Tobi, J.C.A.[149]

"A situation where a member of our honourable profession would, in the middle of prosecuting a civil claim in court, refuse to proceed further and walk out of the case on the ground that a reasonable deposit against his fees by his client was not made is to say the least unethical and not in the best spirit of the profession of law."

George Adesola Oguntade, J.C.A.[150]

"Facts are inimitable stories surrounding a case and on which the most if not all cases depend; are the fountain heads or spring board of law. The tool or the magic that should be in the possession of a seasoned advocate is the mastery of the facts of the case."

Ignatius Chukwudi Pats-Acholonu, J.S.C.[151]

---

[148] Edozien v. Edozien (1993) 1 NWLR (Pt.272) 678 at 693, D
[149] Dahuwa v. Adeniran (1993) 2 NWLR (Pt.277) 580 at 287, F
[150] Owena Bank (Nig.) Plc v. Adedeji (2000) 7 NWLR (Pt.666) 609 at 631, D-E
[151] Obasi Bros Co. Ltd v. MBAS Ltd (2005) 9 NWLR (Pt.929) 117 at pages 133, H and 134, D

"Counsel should guard their tongues and pens in and out of court in their references to judgments of court, particularly as impolite remarks serve no useful purpose except to reduce the integrity of the court before litigants, and this does not augur well for the legal profession."

Amina Adamu Augie, J.C.A.[152]

"It is part of good advocacy for counsel to see Judges as parties in the same boat of administering justice and that both are indispensable parties in that boat."

Niki Tobi, J.C.A.[153]

"...the barrister as an advocate is a minister of justice equally with the judge and he is bound by share industry to place at the disposal of the judge all enactments which are relevant to the case before him."

Owolabi Kolawole, J.C.A.[154]

"To turn notice of appeal into a prose writing with a view to impressing or conveying to the court the intention of the appellant by way of long winding essay is to miss the grammar of notice of appeal. Brevity is the watch word.

Ignatius Chukwudi Pats-Acholonu, J.C.A.[155]

"As an advocate he is a minister of Justice equally with the Judge. He has a monopoly of audience in the High Courts... He has a duty to the court which is paramount... He owes allegiance to a higher cause. It is the cause of truth and justice..."

Victor James Obanua Chigbue, J.C.A.[156]

---

[152] Ayorinde v. Kuforiji (2007) 4 NWLR (Pt.1024) 341 at 373, F-G
[153] Udoh v. State (1994) 2 NWLR (Pt.329) 666 at 685, E-F
[154] Nwadiaro v. Shell Dev. Co. Ltd (1990) 5 NWLR (Pt.150) 322 at 336, A
[155] UBA Plc v. Coker (1996) 4 NWLR (Pt.441) 239 at 247, G
[156] Ekanem v. Akpan (1991) 8 NWLR (Pt.211) 616 at 634, B quoting a restatement of the duties counsel owes to the court in Rondel v. W (1966) 3. All ER 657/665-668

"While I agree that counsel owe their clients a duty to present the best standard of advocacy with a view to obtaining victory, this should not be achieved at the expense of the reputation and integrity of the Judge."

Niki Tobi, J.C.A.[157]

"A counsel who is unable to attend the court owes it a duty to arrange for another counsel to hold his brief. It is discourteous and impolite for a counsel to turn down the invitation of this court to address it further on any issue. If counsel appreciates he is first and foremost an officer of the court, his duty as an officer is to show utmost respect and not treat the process of court with levity."

Olajide Olatawura, J.S.C.[158]

"Lawyers by their very calling are priests in the temple of justice and it behoves of all counsel in that temple to help courts by well researched brief."

Ignatius Chukwudi Pats-Acholonu, J.C.A.[159]

"It is sad and disheartening that a member of the Bar in the last decade of the 21st century still believes in mysticism and nonsense so much so as to postulate that it was responsible for killing a human being. Such a belief, to my mind is not only undesirable but also preposterous."

Isa Ayo Salami, J.C.A.[160]

"In the administration of justice, the courts have not the liberty to act on instinct... Admittedly, intuitive perception, coming

---

[157] Agwuna III v. Isiadinso (1996) 5 NWLR (Pt.451) 705 at 719, C
[158] LSDPC v. Nig. Land and See Foods Ltd (1992) 5 NWLR (Pt.244) 653 at 673, A
[159] Okoroafor v. The Misc. Offence Tribunal (1995) 4 NWLR (Pt.387) 59 at 77, H
[160] Ajidahun v. State (1991) 9 NWLR (Pt.213) 33 at 54, F

from the sub-conscious, often provides the right answer; but such answer not having been arrived at by the recognized Judicial process has no evidential value and serves no useful purpose."

Ephraim Omorose Ibukun Akpata, J.S.C.[161]

"Counsel who calls on a court to overrule its earlier decision has a herculean task to satisfy the court that the decision is wrong. He must show that the decision has caused or perpetuated injustice through the *doctrine of stare decisis* or it has impeded the development of the law or is in fact against public policy or the decision was given *per incuriam*."

Niki Tobi, J.S.C.[162]

"…. all facts are not equal. …when such fact of quality which can literally overwhelm an opposing party are in the grasp of a great lawyer, the elegance or romance of forensic advocacy is easily discernible and it makes a great difference. Facts are like magnets and have the potential to completely turn a seemingly ugly case to a good case. We must never neglect the Roman aphorism *"ex facto oritur jus"* that the law has its offspring on the fact."

Ignatius Chukwudi Pats-Acholonu, J.S.C.[163]

"In the zealousness of counsel to win a case, he must not be over zealous. I say no more in the hope that my message will get to the younger members of the profession."

Eugene Chukwuemeka Ubaezonu, J.C.A.[164]

---

[161] Katto v. CBN (1991) 9 NWLR (Pt.214) 126 at 145, G-H
[162] Awuse v. Odili (2003) 18 NWLR (Pt.851) 116 at 179, C
[163] A-G., Anambra State v. A-G., Federation (2005) 9 NWLR (Pt.931) 572 at 638, H
[164] Mba v. Mba (1999) 10 NWLR (Pt.623) 503 at 513, D

"Certainly, where a legal practitioner without justification holds on to his client's money, all right thinking members of the legal profession must view such a misconduct with great concern not only for the protection of the public, but also for the protection and preservation of the good name of the legal profession."

Mahmud Mohammed, J.S.C.[165]

"Counsel, as partners in the administration of justice, are expected not to disparage the trial conduct of a judge just for the fun of it."

Niki Tobi, J.C.A.[166]

"…Counsel should assiduously cross-check facts placed at their disposal by their over-zealous clients, particularly when such averments are not only far-reaching consequences but moreso when they impinge or appear to impinge on impropriety on the exalted position of the bench."

Okay Achike, J.C.A.[167]

"Counsel have no business to coin out their own expression completely outside the contemplation of the enabling law. That will certainly bring so much confusion in the judicial process… All legal actions are expected to be exact and precise; election petition more so, as they are distinct and separate class of their own, carving out for themselves a contextual uniqueness and a flavour."

Niki Tobi, J.C.A.[168]

---

[165] Ndokwu v. LPDC (2007) 5 NWLR (Pt.1026) 1 at 48, E
[166] National Bank of Nig. Ltd v. Opeola (1994) 1 NWLR (Pt.319) 126 at 141, H
[167] Onigbede v. Balogun (1998) 4 NWLR (Pt.545) 281 at 291, C
[168] Basheer v. Same (1992) 4 NWLR (Pt.236) 491 at 507, E-F

"I think it is undesirable for a barrister to put himself into a situation in which he cannot be 'counsel'; the true sense of the word, because he is in substance the party..."

Sir Adetokunbo Ademola, C.J.N.[169]

"The Constitution can never be seen to be protecting the use of judicial process to undermine respect for law and order and the integrity of the courts. Any action or course of conduct that is seen designed to introduce anarchy into the judicial system must be dealt with appropriately."

Emmanuel Olayinka Ayoola, J.C.A.[170]

"It is unethical for counsel to appear in court without the relevant case file. It is like a carpenter going to his workshop without the requisite wood. As the carpenter cannot carry out his function of carpentry, so also will the advocate not be able to carry out his function of advocacy."

Niki Tobi, J.C.A.[171]

"Counsel conducting a case is, as a matter of law and civil procedure, in complete control of his case and he is a master in his own house."

Sylvester Umaru Onu, J.S.C.[172]

"Indeed, it is proper to observe that where practitioners in the temple of justice refrain from observing the Rule of Law, what right, I ask, have we to complain about refusal of government and others who are so minded, when they ignore or refuse to comply

---

[169] Ojiebge v. Ubani (1961) 2 NSCC 153 at 154
[170] Globe Motors Holdings Ltd v. Honda Motor Co. Ltd (1998) 5 NWLR (Pt.550) 373 at 381, F
[171] Madu v. Okeke (1998) 5 NWLR (Pt.548) 159 at 164, E-F
[172] Akpan v. Utin (1996) 7 NWLR (Pt.463) 634 at 672, C

with orders given by the courts of the land. I believe that the old adage still stands true, viz "Obey first and then complain."

Akintola Olufemi Ejiwunmi, J.C.A.[173]

"Counsel are not underlings to any court or judge. Each side has its role to perform in the dispensation of justice. One side cannot engage in the role of the other. The court or judge hears and decides a case. The counsel presents their clients' aspect of a case. They cannot as a rule directly or indirectly be subjected by the court or judge to defending their integrity as to their right to appear for a client by compelling them to show evidence. Their right of audience cannot be questioned or curtailed in that manner. They are ministers in the Temple of Justice whose absence therefrom affects the ability of the courts to do justice but rather whose presence is the first reassuring sign to further it."

Samson Odemwingie Uwaifo, J.C.A.[174]

"The moment a trial Judge leaves his exalted and independent position that the law has 'sacredly' placed him and moves into the arena of the contest by asking probing and searching questions with a view to finding for one of the parties and therefore against the other party, an appellate court will certainly intervene in favour of the party who is a victim of the Judge's questions."

Niki Tobi, J.C.A.[175]

"In the interest of justice, the trial Judge should, in our adversary type of legal system, as much as possible, remain the umpire or referee in the legal battle between the parties. That measure of independence conjures a considerable degree of respectability

---

[173] Orakwute v. Agagwu (1996) 8 NWLR (Pt.466) 359 at 376, H
[174] Salim v. Ifenkwe (1996) 5 NWLR (Pt.450) 564 at 585-586, H-A
[175] Oteju v. Oluguna (1992) 8 NWLR (Pt.262) 752 at 767, B-C

for, and acceptability of, the judgments or orders or declarations handed down by the courts."
Okay Achike, J.C.A.[176]

"A court does not go on a voyage of speculation imagining things which either happened or might have happened or did not happen."
Eugene Chukwuemeka Ubaezonu, J.C.A.[177]

"...every Judge has a duty to contribute to the development of the law and as long as he does this within the established rules of *stare decisis* he cannot be faulted."
Niki Tobi, J.C.A.[178]

"It must be clearly understood that when a case is thoroughly bad no amount of advocacy on the part of counsel can make it a good one or turn the tide unless of course the plaintiff goofed or so hopelessly mismanaged his case by a demonstration of such unbridled stupidity and incompetence that it throws away carelessly what is within its grip."
Ignatius Chukwudi Pats-Acholonu, J.C.A.[179]

"A legal practitioner is a minister of justice. He is sometimes referred to in a rather expressive manner as a minister in the temple of justice. His first duty therefore is to act in the interest and promotion of justice. That is what sustains his profession and makes it honourable. That is how he earns and maintains his esteem."
Samson Odemwingie Uwaifo, J.C.A.[180]

---

[176] Olawuyi v. Adeyemi (1990) 4 NWLR (Pt.147) 746 at 779, H
[177] Coker v. Adetayo (1992) 6 NWLR (Pt.249) 612 at 625, G-H
[178] Busari v. Oseni (1992) 4 NWLR (Pt.237) 557 at 592, B-C
[179] Greenbelt Ref. Ltd v. FBN Plc (1996) 6 NWLR (Pt.455) 502 at 506, G
[180] Seismograph Services v. Mark (1993) 7 NWLR (Pt.304) 203 at 215, H-A

"Counsel qua counsel, and as an officer of the court, like the trial court, has a responsibility to assist fearlessly in the resolution of the matter in controversy between the parties… There is no gain saying the fact that a timid counsel is a disservice to the court and the profession. In short, instead of being a catalyst to legal development he is bound to exude negative influence in this regard."

Okay Achike, J.C.A.[181]

"It is essential to emphasize that while access to court is an undeniable right of a citizen in a free society, it is the duty of a counsel to examine all facts made available to him painstakingly to avoid a ride to the court that produces failure and disillusionments. A thorough grasp of the facts of the case presented by one with mastery of forensic advocacy is important."

Ignatius Chukwudi Pats-Acholonu, J.S.C.[182]

"Whenever counsel is in some fix or dilemma, they find the principle of law that the mistake of counsel should not be visited on his client, most useful, which they think can do all the magic. Most times, they recite the principle like a kindergarten rhyme or recitation and with confidence that the court will react in their favour."

Niki Tobi, J.C.A.[183]

"Good briefs are pleasant to the courts. They make the work of the court easy and simple. On the other hand, bad briefs can be

---

[181] Okolo v. UBN Ltd (1998) 2 NWLR (Pt.539) 618 at 660, A
[182] IMNL v. Nwachukwu (2004) 13 NWLR (Pt.891) 543 at 570-571, H-A
[183] Lenas Fibreglass Ltd v. Furtado (1997) 5 NWLR (Pt.504) 220 at 236, C

quite irksome and they tend to complicate the work of the court. Bad briefs give the judges sleepless nights."

Eugene Chukwuemeka Ubaezonu, J.C.A.[184]

"... a virile Bar is a great asset to the profession and the court, and should be much encouraged; nevertheless, advocacy popularized by vituperative, unguarded and uncivil language unleashed on the Bench should be roundly deprecated."

Okay Achike, J.C.A.[185]

"An experienced advocate should master the facts of the case very well and put them on the scale before approaching the court. He should seek to make an intellectualized and forensic analysis of the facts ..."

Ignatius Chukwudi Pats-Acholonu, J.C.A.[186]

"...counsel owe the administration of justice and the judicial process a duty to give the traditional professional regard and respect to the Judge, who is the judex in matters before him."

Niki Tobi, J.C.A.[187]

"It cannot be over-emphasized that in-as-much as counsel, and indeed, academicians are fully entitled to review and if necessary to criticize, inappropriate cases, any judgments of all courts of law, inclusive of this court, as they may deem fit, it ought to be admonished that such criticisms must not only be constructive but must be based prima facie on some modicum of clarity of thought, if not scholarship.

Anthony Ikechukwu Iguh, J.S.C.[188]

---

[184] Weide & Co. (Nig.) Ltd v. Weide & Co Hamburg (1992) 6 NWLR (Pt.249) 627 at 641
[185] Okolo v. UBN Ltd. (1998) 2 NWLR (Pt.539) 618 at 661, A
[186] Sirpi Alusteel Const. (Nig.) Ltd v. Snig (Nig.) Ltd (2000) 2 NWLR (Pt.644) 229 at 240, F-G
[187] Schmidt v. Umanah (1997) 1 NWLR (Pt.479) 75 at 83, C
[188] Okino v. Obanebira (1999) 13 NWLR (Pt.636) 535 at 556, F-G

"It is most dangerous precedent for counsel to suspect every judicial conduct of a Judge and rush to negative conclusions capable of tarnishing or spoiling his image or integrity. I think it is in the overall interest of the administration of justice for both the Bar and the Bench to have reciprocal confidence in their different professional abilities in the enforcement of the judicial process."

Niki Tobi, J.C.A.[189]

"Every Nigerian, high or low, (those "Ministers in the Temple of Justice" (justices); the "worshippers" therein, counsel, of course, by no means excepted) owes it to himself and to Nigeria ... to ever work hard enough, stretch himself to the fullest, to live for Nigeria to enable Nigeria live to achieve its highest height in the comity of Nations."

Sylvanus Adiewere Nsofor, J.C.A.[190]

"It is sad, extremely sad, that counsel has the courage to come before the court of law describing the judgment of another court of law as so-called. I must confess that I have never come across such a language in my short life on the bench, and I am not very happy about it. The Nigerian Legal System is a highly civilised one operated by a highly civilised profession of the Bench and the Bar, jointly committed to the use of highly civilised language..."

Niki Tobi, J.C.A.[191]

"Law, they say, is an ass not minding who will ride upon its back and to which direction he will drive it. All that is known is that it is not a respecter of persons. The position of the law will

---

[189] University of Calabar v. Esiaga (1997) 4 NWLR (Pt.502) 719 at 746, B-C
[190] Mil. Admin, Delta State v. Olu of Warri (1997) 7 NWLR (Pt.513) 430 at 466-467 H-A
[191] Menakaya v. Menakaya (1996) 9 NWLR (Pt.472) 256 at 304, G-H

not change. Where it is valid it remains to be so irrespective of whether it misleads anybody or not."

Ibrahim Tanko Muhammad, J.S.C.[192]

"The behaviour of a counsel who at a trial resorted to numerous and unnecessary applications as delaying tactics must in no uncertain terms be deprecated and this court will not lend itself to approving such unbecoming behaviour."

Anthony Ikechukwu Iguh, J.S.C.[193]

"...when counsel states that he was speaking from the Bar it is taken as the gospel truth and woe betides the legal profession when judges take statement of counsel with mistrust."

Moronkeji Omotayo Onalaja, J.C.A.[194]

---

[192] Okpe v. Fan Milk Plc (2017) 2 NWLR (Pt.1549) 282 at 310, F
[193] Olumesan v. Ogundepo (1996) 2 NWLR (Pt.433) 628 at 651, D quoting Fanz Holdings Ltd v. Mrs. Lamotte (1977) NNLR 163 at 168
[194] Opara v. Chinda (1996) 2 NWLR (Pt.432) 527 at 538, A-B

3 ROLE OF THE COURT IN SOCIETY

"The court will not leave a victim of injustice helpless and without a remedy."
Kudirat Motonmori Olatokunbo Kekere Ekun J.S.C.[195]

"The judiciary is not designed as an engine to perpetuate injustice, oppression or impunity and will always resist efforts by anyone to so use it".
Walter Samuel Nkanu Onnoghen, C.J.N.[196]

"...The court has a social duty to help in sounding a note of warning and frowning at criminals who think that the long arm of the law would not get them."
Uzo I. Ndukwe-Anyanwu, J.C.A.[197]

"Courts are to depict substance and justice on the merit and be wary of sacrificing justice on account of technicality."
Clara Bata Ogunbiyi, J.S.C.[198]

"It must be borne in mind that implicit in the judgment of any court is the fact that the public will carefully, mercilessly and pitilessly scrutinize, and methodically weigh any judgment given to discern whether it is in accord with fair play as could be acceptable to the right thinking members of the society."
Ignatius Chukwudi Pats-Acholonu, J.C.A.[199]

---

[195] Lau v. P.D.P 4 NWLR (2018) 6 NWLR (Pt.1608) 60 at127, D-E
[196] Bulet Int'l (Nig.) Ltd v. Olaniyi (2017) 17 NWLR (Pt.1594) 260 at 294, D-E
[197] Nwude v. F.R.N. (2016) 5 NWLR (Pt.1506) 471 at 515, A-B
[198] Agusiobo v. Onyekwelu (2003) 14 NWLR (Pt.839) 34 at 52, H
[199] Fawhinmi v. Akilu (1994) 6 NWLR (Pt.351) 387at 474, B-C

"The court is the primary custodian of the Constitution. It must therefore guard jealously all the provisions of the Constitution and cannot close its eyes to the infringement of the Constitution."

Suleiman Galadima, J.C.A.[200]

"The moment a trial Judge is tempted to asking a question, he should quickly first pose a silent question to himself whether in the process he will not be making a case not made by the other party for the party in which the answer to the question will favour, to the extent that judgment will be given to him. The moment the answer to that silent question is in the affirmative, he should quickly drop the idea and refrain from asking the question."

Niki Tobi, J.C.A.[201]

"A non-suit is not a favour to either side. It is not meant to rob a party of a technical success but it is based on the foundation of justice itself that the door of the temple of justice should not be shut against a party who has not totally failed to prove his case."

Olajide Olatawura, J.S.C.[202]

"A court of law is established to deal with live issues and live matters before it. A court of law is not established to deal with 'ifs'. A court of law is not established to deal with hypothetical matters. A court of law generally has no jurisdiction to anticipate a possible human conduct ... and suddenly push in an order like a flash light. Such order cannot hold in law as it will be hanging in the air like a balloon or like a child's toy."

Niki Tobi, J.C.A.[203]

---

[200] Alamieyeseigha v. Igoniwari (No.2) (2007) 7 NWLR (Pt.1034) 524 at 577, C
[201] Oteju v. Oluguna (1992) 8 NWLR (Pt.262) 752 at 767, F-G
[202] Ugbodume v. Abiegbe (1991) 8 NWLR (Pt.209) 261 at 275
[203] Madike v. State (1992) 8 NWLR (Pt.257) 85 at 103, D

"Law which is strictly applied and not interspersed with equity is no justice but a denial of justice... our Courts are courts of justice not courts of technicality."
Rabiu Danlami Muhammad, J.C.A.[204]

"The Courts are weak and have only judgments. But they remain without argument the main bulwark against authoritarianism in a society which espouses the Rule of Law. To ignore judgments and orders of Courts is to lay a sure foundation for despotism and anarchy."
Augustine Nnamani, J.S.C.[205]

"Accessibility to a court of law to vent a real or imagined grievance is generally regarded as a hallmark of democracy."
Pius Olayiwola Aderemi, J.C.A.[206]

"The court is entitled to protect its person and integrity from being abused. The court as a very busy institution has little or no time for frivolity and vexatiousness."
Niki Tobi, J.C.A.[207]

"The court, particularly an appellate court, cannot stand aloof and watch with insensitivity the legal rights of the parties being plunged into a quagmire or grounded in a state of impasse."
Okay Achike, J.C.A.[208]

"...in the judicial process both counsel and the courts are joint partners in the search for justice, the bedrock of any legal system built on the tenets of democracy and the rule of law. It

---
[204] Merotohun v. State (1992) 7 NWLR (Pt.254) 443 at 451, F
[205] Abaye v. Ofili (1986) 1 NWLR (Pt.15) 134 at 160, G
[206] Unifam Ind. Ltd v. Oceanic Bank Inter'l (Nig.) Ltd (2005) 3 NWLR (Pt.911) 83 at 97, E
[207] Ndoma-Egba v. Govt., Cross River State (1991) 4 NWLR (Pt.188) 773 at 789, H
[208] Dantata & Sawoe Const. v. Egbe (1993)4 NWLR (Pt.287) 335 at 345, E

is in the interest of justice that we all adhere and pursue that neither counsel nor the courts undercut, outsmart or discredit one another. And this is more when neither can exist without the other. And that is why they are joint partners in progress, not in the sense of corporate entity though."

Niki Tobi, J.C.A.[209]

"Self-help by itself is a primitive remedy capable of causing a breach of peace."

Paul Kemdilim Nwokedi, J.S.C.[210]

"In these days of global recession, punctuated with the biting economy, arising from the daily racing inflation, the judgment debtor usually wins the sympathy of the court, but the sympathy should not be carried to a ridiculous extent, to make nonsense of the judgment of the court."

Niki Tobi, J.C.A.[211]

"It is common knowledge that the much-vaunted desire to gain speed in our adversary adjudicatory system invariably results in undue tardiness and loss of speed and time. Judges should exercise a lot of restraint in determining cases prematurely in limine. Such 'accelerated' hearings leave a lot to be desired in the consideration of ordinary independent or impartial observer. They must be heeded. This court cannot sanction injustice by the short-circuit of technicality."

Okay Achike, J.C.A.[212]

---

[209] UBA Ltd v. Taan (1993) 4 NWLR (Pt.287) 368 at 381, D
[210] Agbai v. Okogbue (1991) 7 NWLR (Pt.204) 391 at 417, D
[211] ACB Ltd v. Nnamani (1991) 4 NWLR (Pt.186) 486 at 495, E-F
[212] Ani v. Nna (1996) 4 NWLR (Pt.440) 101 at 126, C-D

"...the court must be guided by the interest of the parties, applying the usual generic and vague, though inevitable overall interest of justice test."

Niki Tobi, J.C.A.[213]

"The judge must remain impartial in the correction of errors made by a party in the case before him...Impartial detachment should be his guide words...This does not mean that he must keep his vision clouded in the nature of the proverbial blind-folded justice. Clear to see where the truth lies; the less dust there is, the better."

Adolphus Godwin Karibi-Whyte, J.S.C.[214]

"One of the highly treasured qualities of a good Judge in this country and indeed in any common law jurisdiction is that of impartiality. Once the litigating public casts some aspersions or doubt on the quality of a Judge in terms of impartiality or partiality, the opposite of impartiality, with a view to disparaging his person as a Judge qua judex, then the entire administration of justice runs into some trouble."

Niki Tobi, J.C.A.[215]

"It is essential that the court should never embark on resolving issues on mere contrasting affidavits as there are present dangers that it would become inextricably involved in the quagmire of the matter and might decide the main issue in the suit due to much forage into the grey areas of the case."

Ignatius Chukwudi Pats-Acholonu, J.C.A.[216]

---

[213] ACB Ltd v. Nnamani (1991) 4 NWLR (Pt.186) 486 at 496, E
[214] Akinbinu v. Oseni (1992) 1 NWLR (Pt.215) 97 at 121-122, H-A
[215] REAN Ltd v. Aswani Textiles Ltd (1991) 2 NWLR (Pt.176) 639 at 665, F-G
[216] UBA v. Onagoruwa (1996) 3 NWLR (Pt.439) 700 at 708, B

"...a court of law is not a charitable organization that may give or donate beyond what is asked for.... To go beyond that would be going against the Principle of Law that a litigant does not get what he does not claim."

Aloma Mariam Mukhtar, J.S.C.[217]

"Gone are the eras in the development of law of equity when equity was so fluid and intractable in its content, so much so that despite the crystalization of principles of equity into a body of discernable rules, it was generally said that the contents of rules of equity were 'as long as the Chancellor's foot'."

Okay Achike, J.C.A.[218]

"The court is and must be run as a solemn, dignified and civilized forum where the sacred duty of the administration of justice is carried out with consistent sobriety of the mind. It is not a pandemonium from where insults are shouted. That will surely have the consequence of discrediting the judiciary and bringing it into disrepute. Any judge who does so is an agent of such odium."

Samson Odemwingie Uwaifo, J.C.A.[219]

"Respect begets respect. It is really shocking for a Judge to treat counsel appearing before him with disrespect... The judicial powers granted to a Court are not personal powers to be used arbitrarily or personally. The powers belong to the court."

Ignatius Chukwudi Pats-Acholonu, J.C.A.[220]

---

[217] Eyibagbe v. Eyibagbe (1996) 1 NWLR (Pt.425) 408 at 415, D
[218] Chukwuma v. Chukwuma (1996) 1 NWLR (Pt.426) 543 at 553, E-F
[219] Salim v. Ifenkwe (1996) 5 NWLR (Pt.450) 564 at 586, E-F
[220] Salim v. Ifenkwe (1996) 5 NWLR (Pt.450) 564 at 587, B

"What the court must do as part of its primary duty to assist justice to triumph is to ensure that any technicality which might be an obstacle is got rid of. That will be consistent with the trend that the time is no more when disputes are dealt with rather on technicalities than on the merits."

Samson Odemwingie Uwaifo, J.C.A.[221]

"A relief which is the show piece or fulcrum upon which the entire litigation rests, cannot admit verbose or rigmarole language. A relief cannot camp with any form of ambiguity. They cannot go together."

Niki Tobi, J.C.A.[222]

"The courts have warned time without number that parties should not throw to the wind the wisdom of leaving the prosecution of issues or points that can be taken advantageously after the final decision of the High Court in an appeal to the Court of Appeal till the High Court has given its final decision and appeal against the decision lodged…"

Dennis Onyejife Edozie, J.C.A.[223]

"…for the court to describe a party by using a base language in calling him a faceless intervener - a term denoting one without honours and having mendacious behaviour is to my mind to use the highly esteemed position of the bench to harass one who seeks justice in the Temple of Justice."

Ignatius Chukwudi Pats-Acholonu, J.C.A.[224]

---

[221] Jamin Systems Consultants Ltd v. Braithwaite (1996) 5 NWLR (Pt.449) 459 at 470, C
[222] Ajikawo v. Ansaldo (Nig.) Ltd (1991) 2 NWLR (Pt.173) 359 at 374, C
[223] Gomwalk v. Okwuosa (1996) 3 NWLR (Pt.439) 681 at 691, G-H
[224] Salim v. Ifenkwe (1996) 5 NWLR (Pt.450) 564 at 587, B

"...the learned Judge as the depository of the law, the living oracle, is bound by an oath to decide according to the law of the land ..."

Owolabi Kolawole, J.C.A.[225]

"I make bold to say that the integrity of counsel, qua counsel, and who speaks from the bar has, as a matter of professional convention and etiquette at the bar, seldomly been called to question. We, as Judges, who have passed through the crucible, should not overtly or covertly, lend support to destroy that convention which is the pride of our profession in terms of its respectability, integrity and honour."

Okay Achike, J.C.A.[226]

"...documents generally do not lie, and even when they lie as a result of fraudulent human intervention, they lie less than the mouth and lips of the human being...Certainly, a court of law will be nearer the truth if not at the real hilt of truth to fall back on the document rather than the affidavit evidence which could be tutored or tailored in proof of the case of the particular deponent."

Niki Tobi, J.C.A.[227]

"A suit is academic where it is merely theoretical, makes empty sound, and of no practical utilitarian value to the plaintiff even if judgment is given in his favour. A suit is academic if it is not related to practical situation of human nature and humanity."

Niki Tobi, J.S.C.[228]

---

[225] Nwadiaro v. Shell Dev. Co. Ltd (1990) 5 NWLR (Pt.150) 322 at 335, G
[226] Princewill v. Usman (1990) 5 NWLR (Pt.150) 274 at 282, G-H
[227] Oyefeso v. Omogbehin (1991) 4 NWLR (Pt.187) 596 at 614-615, H-A
[228] Plateau State v. A.G., Federation (2006) 3 NWLR (Pt.967) 346 at 419, G

"...it is a dangerous practice for the court to formulate issues for the parties. It is within the province of the parties to indicate the issues they wish the court to resolve and the court taking upon itself the formulation of issues for the parties may unwittingly be setting a destructive trap for itself to be accused of jumping into the fray but forcing issues down the parties' throats."
Salihu Modibbo Alfa Belgore, J.S.C.[229]

"... When an authority is used in disregard of the facts of a case, the doctrine of judicial precedent no more creates a sense of certainty but a moribund state of the law through the indiscriminate use of its established principles the law will refuse to grow. It cannot settle live issues. Then robotism would have been installed as machine for the administration of justice. It would all end in inevitable confusion and uncertainty."
Samson Odemwingie Uwaifo, J.C.A.[230]

"A Judge is an impartial umpire between the parties; ...He must not venture into unnecessary and untenable technicality so as to close the avenue of redressing the grievances sought by the disputants."
Ibrahim Kolapo Sulu-Gambari, J.C.A.[231]

"The context of the rules of natural justice is not stereotyped and a duty to act judicially does not necessarily connote an obligation to observe the procedural and evidential rules of court of law."
Ignatius Chukwudi Pats-Acholonu, J.C.A[232]

---

[229] Nwokoro v. Onuma (1990) 3 NWLR (Pt.136) 22 at 35, H
[230] Iwuno v. Dieli (1990) 5 NWLR (Pt.149) 126 at 134-135, H-B
[231] Ajileye v. Fakayode (1990) 5 NWLR (Pt.148) 92 at 100-101, H-A
[232] Edet v. Chief of Staff (1994) 2 NWLR (Pt. 324) 41 at 60E-F quoting Halsbury's Laws of England, 4th Edition (Vol.1) at p. 80 para 66

"Certainly, self-help has no place in our civilized world as it is clearly against the rule of law in a democracy."

Niki Tobi, J.S.C[233]

"This court will never allow a party before it to steal a match on his adversary."

Philip Nnaemeka-Agu, J.S.C[234]

"Customary law is the organic or living law of the indigenous people of Nigeria regulating their lives and transactions. It is organic in that it is not static. It is regulatory in that it controls the lives and transactions of the community subject to it. I would say that customary law goes further and imports justice to the lives of all those subject to it."

Andrews Otutu Obaseki, J.S.C[235]

"Apart from the constitutional and statutory protections to certain parties and litigants, we as Judges, should be upright in our adjudicatory functions across the board, come rain, come sunshine. Our only interest should be doing justice to the parties through law."

Niki Tobi, J.C.A[236]

"It saves valuable time and reduced the cost of litigation to remove the weeds of irrelevancies and cob-webs of matters unnecessarily beclouding otherwise clear issues."

Adolphus Godwin Karibi-Whyte, J.S.C[237]

---

[233] Okochi v. Animkwoi (2003) 18 NWLR (Pt. 851) 1 at 28, E
[234] Olaniyi v. Aroyehun (1991) 5 NWLR (Pt.194) 652 at 687, E
[235] Oyewunmi v. Ogunesan (1990) 3 NWLR (Pt.137) 182 at 207, E-F
[236] Onagoruwa v. IGP (1991) 5 NWLR (Pt.193) 593 at 650, B
[237] Bamgboye v. Olarewaju (1991) 4 NWLR (Pt.184) 132 at 151, G

"For the Courts to take part in any manner to decide which member of a Party is properly nominated for election or not is to put themselves in the thick of an undesirable political imbroglio. It is likely to destabilise the judiciary."

Samson Odemwingie Uwaifo, J.C.A[238]

"It has now become almost an axiom or an aphorism in our judicial system to say that a discretionary power must be exercised not only judicially but also judiciously."

Niki Tobi, J.C.A[239]

"The situation in this case looks to me like the case of two sons of one father who each wants to go out wearing their father's hat. These children quarrel and fight over who wears the hat while their father is sitting in the house holding his hat. Common sense dictates that the proper person to decide which one wears that hat is their father, not any outsider..."

Victor James Obanua Chigbue, J.C.A[240]

"...there is nothing sacrosanct or magical in a word, including the notorious appellate language of "the learned trial Judge erred in law". On no account should a court of law be hypnotized or carried away by that expression, which by virtue of frequent usage in our appellate system has become more of a cliché or axiom, rather than conveying the real position of the appeal."

Niki Tobi, J.C.A.[241]

---

[238] Balonwu v. Chinyelu (1991) 4 NWLR (Pt.183) 30 at 40, G
[239] ACB Ltd. v. Nnamani (1991) 4 NWLR (Pt.186) 486 at 494, G
[240] Balonwu v. Chinyelu (1991) 4 NWLR (Pt.183) 30 at 41, B (quoting with approval the trial judge)
[241] Fumudoh v. Aboro (1991) 9 NWLR (Pt.214) 210 at 231, A

"The justice in conciliation is that of concession to calm the atmosphere and bring peace. It has nothing to do with the rights of the parties according to law."

Andrews Otutu Obaseki, J.S.C.[242]

"...the unbridled use of court processes with an undertone of some mischief calculated to disturb the free flow or smooth dispensation of justice must never be allowed in the citadel of justice, if justice, in the real sense of the word, is to be seen to be done."

Pius Olayiwola Aderemi, J.C.A.[243]

"...the rules of court, like practice directions, are rules touching the administration of justice; they exist for the attainment of justice with ease, certainty and dispatch. They must never be an antithesis of the fundamental principles of justice.

Pius Olayiwola Aderemi, J.C.A.[244]

"A Judge by the nature of his position and professional calling… is the cynosure of the entire adjudication in court, and like Caesar's wife of Ancient Rome, he is expected to live above board and above suspicion if the judicial process should not experience any reverse or suffer any detriment."

Niki Tobi, J.C.A.[245]

"A court and by extension a tribunal is not a Father Christmas and cannot therefore grant a party a relief he has not asked for."

Dennis Onyejife Edozie, J.C.A.[246]

---

[242] Fawehinmi v. NBA (No. 2) (1989) NWLR (Pt.105) 558 at 627
[243] Oteju v. Magma Maritime Services Ltd (2000) 1 NWLR (Pt.640) 270 at 342, D-E
[244] Oteju v. Magma Maritime Services Ltd (2000) 1 NWLR (Pt.640) 270 at 346, A-B
[245] Eribuna v. Obiorah (1999) 8 NWLR (Pt.616) 622 at 643, F
[246] Tanko v. Caleb (1999) 8 NWLR (Pt.616) 606 at 611, A

"The moment right-minded or right-thinking people are of the view that the Judge was biased or there was likelihood of bias, so much violence is done to the fair hearing principles as contained in the Constitution."

Niki Tobi, J.C.A.[247]

"Once a Judge descends into the arena, justice will definitely be impaired and possibly shattered beyond imagination. The duty of a Judge sitting in his exalted throne of justice is to act as an unbiased umpire. He must not deviate in any manner. And any reasonable onlooker in his court should be able to go home smiling and saying - yes the Judge did his job."

John Afolabi Fabiyi, J.C.A.[248]

"...it is rather officious and treading on a perilous path for one to arrogate to oneself the right to choose and pick between court orders in terms of whether they are valid or null and void."

Okay Achike, J.S.C.[249]

"The moment a court of law intends to rewrite a statute or really rewrites a statute, the intention of the lawmaker is thrown overboard and the court changes places with the lawmaker."

Niki Tobi, J.S.C.[250]

"The court is and must be run as a solemn, dignified and civilized forum where the sacred duty of the administration of justice is carried out with a consistent sobriety of the mind."

Samson Odemwingie Uwaifo, J.C.A.[251]

---

[247] Eribuna v. Obiorah (1999) 8 NWLR (Pt.616) 622 at 645, C
[248] Ejimkonye v. State (2000) 3 NWLR (Pt.648) 262 at 272, E-F
[249] Babatunde v. Olatunji (2000) 2 NWLR (Pt.646) 557 at 572, E
[250] Araka v. Egbue (2003) 7 SC 75 at 85
[251] Salim v. Ifenkwe (1996) 5 NWLR (Pt.450) 564 at 586, E

"Trial courts are once again admonished in the strongest possible terms against undue and/or inordinate delay in the determination of suits once the actual hearing of such suits has commenced."

Anthony Ikechukwu Iguh, J.S.C.[252]

"A trial court is not to go on a wild goose chase; to embark on an academic exercise in which all sorts of questions are discussed at will without reference to the pleadings, to the issues and to the admissible evidence."

George Adesola Oguntade, J.C.A.[253]

"The duty of the court is that of an umpire whose duty is to tender the rope and not to step into the brawl by excising argument on good grounds of appeal from those of bad ones."

Isa Ayo Salami, J.C.A.[254]

"There is indeed a duty on the trial court to analyse the evidence of both sides of the dispute, gauge the credibility of the witnesses, ascertain whether or not grave contradictions exist in the evidence to warrant its belief or disbelief and then ultimately ascribe probative value to any piece of such evidence which the court deems deserving such value…. The pendulum of the imaginary scale of justice must contain each and all of the competing sets of evidence and wherever the balance tilts

---

[252] Egbo v. Agbara (1997) 1 NWLR (Pt.481) 293 at 315, F
[253] Nyagba v. Mbanan (1996) 9 NWLR (Pt.471) 207 at 221, F quoting Oputa, J.S.C.in Overseas Construction Ltd v. Creek Enterprise Ltd (1985) 3 NWLR (Pt.13) 407 at 419.
[254] Bello v. Otolorin (1996) 9 NWLR (Pt.470) 49 at 72, C-D quoting himself in the unreported case CA/I/14/92 Madam Asiawu Adeteju Korede v. Prince Adebayo Adedokun & Another delivered on 20th June, 1994.

signifies that the set which has tilted the balance has more weight."
Mahmud Mohammed, J.C.A.[255]

"The attitude of this Court, I believe, has always been that whenever it is possible to determine a case on its merit, the Court should not cling to technicalities."
Idris Legbo Kutigi, J.S.C.[256]

"…All laws that have the machinery of ousting the jurisdiction of the courts particularly in respect of tending to extinguish the powers to adjudicate on matters relating to fundamental rights of citizenry are obnoxious, nefarious, primitive and negation of civilized principle that are enshrined in any civilized jurisprudence."
Ignatius Chukwudi Pats-Acholonu, J.C.A.[257]

"Under Nigerian criminal jurisdiction, the power of a court exercising criminal jurisdiction to convict on alternatives offences or lesser offence is limited and cannot be exercised outside the limits laid down by law."
Dahiru Musdapher, J.S.C.[258]

"A trial is not an investigation, and investigation is not the function of the court. A trial is the public demonstration and testing before a court of the cases of the contending parties."
Muhammed Bello, C.J.N.[259]

---

[255] Rafukka v. Kurfi (1996) 6 NWLR (Pt.453) 235 at 244-245, H-A
[256] Chime v. Ude (1996) 7 NWLR (Pt. 461) 379 at 446, C (in his dissenting opinion)
[257] Kalango v. Governor of Bayelsa (2002) 17 NWLR (Pt.617) at page 633-634, H-A
[258] Nigerian Air Force v. Kalmaldeen (2007) 7 NWLR (Pt.1032) 164 at 190, D
[259] Nwankwo v. State (1985) NCLR 228 at 297

"Instinct, assumption and sentiments have no role to play in adjudication. They are not good premises for adjudication and the court should not indulge in them."

Saka Adeyemi Ibiyeye, J.C.A.[260]

"The constitutional guarantee or right of accessibility to law connotes unlimited opportunity for a citizen to readily seek a remedy or defend a cause in the court of law on the premise he should be given a chance of putting whatever is his case across to the court. This equally means that justice must be even handed. It will indeed be truncated justice where the court or any tribunal of justice resorts to summary trial of a case that is weighty when one of the parties to the case cannot be said to have lost interest in continuing with the trial of the case."

Ignatius Chukwudi Pats-Acholonu, J.C.A.[261]

"Guess work has no place in the adjudicating process, hence where and whenever a party seeks or sets in motion the machinery of justice to quash, nullify or set aside any proceedings or decisions (report inclusive) such a person is under the legal duty to produce or exhibit the report or proceedings before the court."

Tijani Abdullahi, J.C.A.[262]

"A mere speculative observation cannot be a substitute to proof of a fact asserted in a civil suit."

Niki Tobi, J.S.C.[263]

---

[260] Odock v. State (2007) 7 NWLR (Pt.1033) 369 at 399, D and F
[261] Fawhinmi v. Akilu (1994) 6 NWLR (Pt.351) 387at 474, D
[262] Towoju v. Governor of Kwara State (2005) 324 at 350, C-D
[263] Archibong v. Ita (2004) 2 NWLR (Pt.858) 590 at 619H

"The court is not a Father Christmas and has no jurisdiction to make an order which has not been pleaded or prayed for by a litigant."

John Iyang Okoro, J.C.A.[264]

"Such garrulity or needless excitement which makes a judge descend into the arena of trial as though he is a party offends an ethical behaviour expected of a judge and must be avoided as it may upset the delicate balance of the case."

Ignatius Chukwudi Pats-Acholonu, J.C.A.[265]

"...the law as it stands is not predisposed to beneficent philanthropy of doling out bounties on the basis of need rather than supplication that identifies the need. The rule is ask and you shall be given if you are legally qualified for your request."

Sule Aremu Olagunju, J.C.A.[266]

"A case does not lose its value as a judicial precedent on the ground of age. As a matter of law, a case which survived the test of judicial precedent is recognized as stable if decided by the highest court of the land, and will receive the adoration of the lower courts until overruled by the highest court."

Niki Tobi, J.S.C.[267]

"It is the duty of court to use its powers to discover the true intents of the law and do justice and not to destroy them unless the words used convey a meaning that obscure the true intentions of the statute."

Ignatius Chukwudi Pats-Acholonu, J.S.C.[268]

---

[264] Ayorinde v. Kuforiji (2007) 4 NWLR (Pt.1024) 341 at 371, D-E
[265] Ibrahim v. The State (1995) 3 NWLR (Pt.381) 35 at 48, E-F
[266] Ayalogu v. Agu (2002) 3 NWLR (Pt.753) 168 at 184, B-C
[267] Okpala v. Okpu (2003) 5 NWLR (Pt.812) 183 at 215, B-C
[268] Broad Bank of Nig. Ltd v. Olayiwola (2005) 3 NWLR (Pt.912) 434 at 458, H

"...the inherent jurisdiction of the court does not provide a cloak for judicial acrobatics away from the rule of law."
John Afolabi Fabiyi, J.C.A.[269]

"Courts of law, as most serious and sacred institutions, do not build upon hypothesis which is an idea suggested as a possible way of explaining facts or providing arguments. The adjective "hypothetical" really means that which has not been proved or shown to be real. It also connotes imaginary. ... Hypothesis by their very nature generally have no limitations and courts of law by their judgments have limitations."
Niki Tobi, J.S.C.[270]

"...a court seized with the proceedings should not lose sight of the fact that essentially parties go to court in order to obtain justice. It is certainly not the intention of any progressive law to asphyxiate justice and render it obtuse by an interpretation that leaves a party seeking justice empty handed by way of rendition of a judgment on a matter in a very narrow sense."
Ignatius Chukwudi Pats-Acholonu, J.S.C.[271]

"With respect, courts are not known to indulge in legal double-talk."
Christopher Mitchell Chukwuma-Eneh, J.C.A.[272]

"A suit is hypothetical if it is imaginary and not based on real facts. A suit is hypothetical if it looks like a "mirage" to deceive the defendant and the court as to the reality of the cause of action. A suit is a semblance of actuality of the cause of action or relief sought."
Niki Tobi, J.S.C.[273]

---

[269] Guinness (Nig.) Ltd v. Udeani (2000) 14 NWLR (Pt.687) 367 at 395, C
[270] Olafisoye v. Fed. Rep. of Nigeria (2004) 4 NWLR (Pt.864) 580 at 654-655, H-A
[271] Yusufu v. Obasanjo (2003) 16 NWLR (Pt.847) 554 at 639, H
[272] Ushae v. COP (2005) 11NWLR (Pt. 937) 499 at 535, B
[273] Plateau State v. A.G. Federation (2006) 3 NWLR (Pt.967) 346 at 419, H

"A Judge must be very patient and accommodate within the rules of court, the inadequacies of counsel and parties also; otherwise he gives an impression of descending to the arena."
Adrian Chukwuemeka Orah, J.C.A.[274]

"…taking contempt cases first is to demonstrate to the public that the court being the creature of the constitution …. should protect its dignity and not to allow the ubiquitous Legislatures nor the over-bearing Executive, and not even a citizen to brazenly do an act that would diminish the powers duly vested by the Constitution in the administration of justice."
Ignatius Chukwudi Pats-Acholonu, J.S.C.[275]

"…for a trial Judge to intermeddle with a party's exercise of his option in the circumstances would be seen as not maintaining his dignified role as an impartial or unbiased Judge. Worse still he is seen as having chosen to descend into the arena and invariably he may not avoid getting soiled…"
Christopher Mitchell Chukwuma-Eneh, J.C.A.[276]

"No Judge can form his opinion as to the frontiers of Bill of Rights in any democracy and import his pet ideas in the construction of provisions which are clear and obvious in terms of vindicating the freedom of the individuals in society."
Niki Tobi, J.C.A.[277]

"As guardians of the rich tradition of jurisprudence which we have inherited and imbibed, we must make secure the authority of law as the servant of liberty, wisely and culturally conceived

---
[274] FBN Plc v. Ejikeme (1996) 7 NWLR (Pt. 462) 597 at 616, A-B
[275] Ebhodaghe v. Okoye (2004) 18 NWLR (Pt.905) 472 at 495, C-D
[276] Ushae v. COP (2005) 11NWLR (Pt. 937) 499 at 530, C-D
[277] Onwo v. Oko (1996) 6 NWLR (Pt. 456) 584 at 613, E

as the expression of the righteousness which would exalt the law and indirectly this country."

Ignatius Chukwudi Pats-Acholonu, J.C.A.[278]

"…Courts must insist, wherever possible, on the rigid adherence to the Constitution of the land and curb the tendency of those who would like to establish what virtually are kangaroo courts under different guises and smoke screen of judicial regularity. This, the court, in their appointed duties, must sternly endeavour to resist…"

Francis Fedode Tabai, J.S.C.[279]

"A Judge who hears only one side of a case before him and refuses or fails to hear the other side before giving decision has done grave injustice, not only to the party not heard but also to the Constitution, which he swore on that eventful day of his life to 'preserve, protect and defend'."

Niki Tobi, J.C.A.[280]

"Every Judge is an umpire. He must ever keep a cool head, never loose his sense of justice and for no earthly reason appear to give an impression obviously or inadvertently, that he is championing the case of either party no matter the conduct of the party or counsel in a case which can be sometimes nauseating and almost intolerable."

Adrian Chukwuemeka Orah, J.C.A.[281]

---

[278] Okoroafor v. The Miscellaneous Offences Tribunal (1995) 4 NWLR (Pt. 387) 59 at 78, G
[279] Adeogun v. Fashogbon (2008) 17 NWLR (Pt. 1115) 149 at 175E-G re-emphasising the decision of Aniagolu, J.S.C. in Adeyemi (Alafin of Oyo) v. A.-G., Oyo State (1984) 1 SCNLR 525 at 602, G
[280] Emerah v. Chiekwe (1996) 7 NWLR (Pt. 462) 536 at 548, D-E
[281] FBN Plc v. Ejikeme (1996) 7 NWLR (Pt. 462) 597 at 616, B

"Compliance with the orders of court is the very basis of the proper functioning of the court. It is therefore not right and indeed it must not be allowed to germinate in the system that parties and/or their counsel are free to choose when to obey orders of court. It is a violation of the Rule of Law so to do."

Akintola Olufemi Ejiwunmi, J.C.A.[282]

"Gone are the days and they are almost out of human memory when the courts dichotomized between judicial acts and administrative acts, as if no water can pass through the demarcation, as it related to the applicability or otherwise of the natural justice rule. The trend changed in 1959 ... and since then the English courts have held in appropriate cases that certiorari will apply to quash administrative acts where the rules of natural justice are not complied with."

Niki Tobi, J.C.A.[283]

"The Court guards its power and image jealously. It should therefore be extremely wary in the manner it exposes such image, the diminution of its powers and the enforcement of its authority to public ridicule."

Adolphus Godwin Karibi-Whyte, J.S.C.[284]

"The courts are courts of law but may the day never come when they cease to be courts of justice. Substantial justice cannot be done unless courts of justice strain to ensure that appeals are heard on the merit."

Augustine Nnamani, J.S.C.[285]

---

[282] Orakwute v. Agagwu (1996) 8 NWLR (Pt. 466) 359 at 376, G-H
[283] Steel Bell (Nig.) Ltd v. Govt. of Cross River State (1996) 3 NWLR (Pt.438) 571 at 589, C-D
[284] Odogwu v. Odogwu (1992) 2 NWLR (Pt.225) 539 at 558, H
[285] Erisi v. Idika (No.1) (1987) 4 NWLR (Pt.66) 503

"Care should be taken by the court always not to sacrifice justice on the altar of technicalities. The time is no more when disputes are dealt with rather on technicalities and not on the merit... To be otherwise, would set in motion a system that would encourage technicalities to take over the rules of court. This will be going back to the middle ages. It will be a retrogressive step, it will end in travesty of justice."

Kayode Eso, J.S.C.[286]

"Courts are not frightened of an ouster clause. They respect it but when an ouster clause seeks to make it impossible for the courts to protect the common man, and make laws which cannot stand the test of reason or that is affront to decency and intelligence, then a court should be careful not to lend weight to a law that would make it enemies of the common man and not the last hope of the common man."

Ignatius Chukwudi Pats-Acholonu, J.C.A.[287]

"No two artists convey exactly the same painting from an assigned object. So too, no two Judges write judgment using exactly the same house style and the same coloration... Judgment writing is not an arithmetical or geometrical exercise which must answer exactly to laid down rules in the field of mathematics."

Niki Tobi, J.S.C.[288]

"...the attitude of the court in this century is doing and deciding cases on substantial justice."

Moronkeji Omotayo Onalaja, J.C.A.[289]

---

[286] Chiwendu v. Mbamali (1980) 3/4 S.C. 31 at 81-82
[287] Okoroafor v. The Miscellaneous Offences Tribunal (1995) 4 NWLR (Pt.387) 59 at 78, D
[288] Usiobaifo v. Usibaifo (2005) 3 NWLR (Pt. 913) 665 at 692, E-G
[289] Pabod Supplies Ltd v. Beredugo (1996) 5 NWLR (Pt. 448)304 at 330, E

"We should avoid circumstances where the courts would become slaves to rules. Motor cars and telephones are essential for ease of transport and communication as they are meant to serve us not vice-versa. If the worst comes to the worst we can do without them."
          Ignatius Chukwudi Pats-Acholonu, J.C.A.[290]

"It must be understood that in a free society, where the concept of the rule of law is the order of the day and where the courts are alive to their duties, it will be setting the clock back if through our conduct we indulge in actions which tend to exclude the other party from being heard."
          Ignatius Chukwudi Pats-Acholonu, J.C.A.[291]

"Compromise judgment being grafted as a species of judicial decision must belong to the world of the chimera; it is a bogey which must be banished from serious contentious judicial deliberations."
          John Afolabi Fabiyi, J.C.A.[292]

"A suit is speculative if it is not supported by facts or very low on facts but very high in guesses. As courts of law are not established to adjudicate on guesses but on facts such actions are struck out."
          Niki Tobi, J.S.C.[293]

"No judge has the right to give a ruling or judgment in annoyance or in anger. That state of mind will certainly be prejudicial to one of the parties, thus hurting the fair hearing principle duly

---

[290] Okpala v. D.G., NCMM (1996)4 NWLR (Pt. 444) 585 at 594, G-H
[291] Credit Alliance Finance Services Ltd v. Mallah (1998) 10 NWLR (Pt. 569) 341 at 351, C-D
[292] Guinness (Nig.) Ltd v. Udeani (2000) 14 NWLR (Pt.687) 367 at 395, C
[293] Plateau State v. A.-G., Federation (2006) 3 NWLR (Pt.967) 346 at 419, G-H

entrenched in the constitution. A judge must keep his mind totally free in the judicial process, and this means that he must disabuse his mind of all possible prejudices and antagonism."
Eugene Chukwuemeka Ubaezonu, J.C.A.[294]

"No doubt a court is often driven to near exasperation by counsel who would not demonstrate the minimum diligence a court should demand, in the conduct of their client's cases, but the reaction of the court in such situations should be global i.e. should also consider the ends of justice to the litigant who would greatly suffer from an order dismissing the case."
George Adesola Oguntade, J.C.A.[295]

"It goes without saying that the content of any law is to secure maximum happiness for the greatest number. Where a legislation so described appears equivocal i.e. in the sense that it is not easy to relate what it seeks to cure with the words used, it will, beremiss of a court to clearly wash its hands off the case because of ouster clause."
Ignatius Chukwudi Pats-Acholonu, J.C.A.[296]

"No matter how good a Judge is at remembering the demeanour of witnesses who have given evidence before him at a trial, it will be asking or expecting too much from a trial Judge to remember the demeanour of each witness called by the parties in a trial that lasted over 14 years. No Jupiter or any Solomon can achieve such a feat."
Atinuke Omobonike Ige, J.C.A.[297]

---

[294] Isamade v. Okei (1998) 2 NWLR (Pt.538) 455 at 468, B-C
[295] Daniang v Teachers Service Commission (1996) 5 NWLR (Pt.446) 96 at 109, B-C
[296] Guardian Newspaper Ltd v. A.G. Federation (1995) 5 NWLR (Pt.398) 703 at 738-739, H-A
[297] Atejioye v. Ayeni (1998) 6 NWLR (Pt.552) 132 at 141C-D

"The court does not readily throw up its hand with abandonement because there exists an ouster clause. It rather examines the issue minutely to discover whether the power of adjudication on the matter had been taken away by the law enacted by the sovereign power."
      Ignatius Chukwudi Pats-Acholonu, J.C.A.[298]

"Both the Judge and counsel are involved in the administration of justice and as such are indispensable and viable partners in progress. They both are out to uphold the rule of law. That is what the two, by their different but most related and complimentary professional callings, have agreed to uphold."
      Niki Tobi, J.C.A.[299]

"A court of law is an umpire in a case and should not allow itself to descend into the arena by conducting itself in such a way as to give the impression that it is biased."
      James Ogenyi Ogebe, J.C.A.[300]

"It is the sacred duty of courts to ensure that everything is done towards the facilitation of the hearing of the matter and the expedition of the hearing of the case."
      Adolphus Godwin Karibi-Whyte, J.S.C.[301]

"The beauty, the elegance and romance of our adjudicatory system is that the court should hear all sides, carefully compare the weight of the evidence given and make a proper appraisal

---

[298] N.I.O. & M. R. v. Okonya (1996) 4 NWLR (Pt.444) 611 at 620 para. H
[299] Orakwute v. Agagwu (1996) 8 NWLR (Pt.466) 359 at 376 para. B
[300] Awodi v. Kagoro (1998) 4 NWLR (Pt.547) 601 at 607 paras. B-C
[301] Alsthom SA v. Saraki (2000) 14 NWLR (Pt.687) 415 at 427 para. B

before determining preponderance after such painstaking considerations of all issues addressed upon it."

Ignatius Chukwudi Pats-Acholonu, J.S.C.[302]

"A Judge in the judicial process is said to be biased if he favours one of the parties to the detriment of the other irrespective of the merits of the case before him. He is prepared to give judgment to the other party he favours at whatever cost. He is blind to the merits of the case as he shows his inclination for the party he favours overtly in the course of the hearing..."

Niki Tobi, J.C.A.[303]

"It is for the court to determine whether it has jurisdiction...For the chairman to take it upon himself to tell the presiding judge where his jurisdiction begins and ends in drug offences related matters is in my opinion a brazen effrontery to assume to be more knowledgeable than the court in law. I am scandalized at the veiled threat to gag the judiciary."

Ignatius Chukwudi Pats-Acholonu, J.C.A.[304]

"The court has no jurisdiction to imprison any process before it or pretend to forget its existence, thus giving it a burial, a most indecent one for that matter. That is not justice. That is clear injustice and it is a very raw one."

Niki Tobi, J.C.A.[305]

"The Judge is seen essentially as an arbiter in conflicts whether between individuals or between individuals and the State and

---

[302] Adebayo v. Shogo (2005) 7 NWLR (Pt.925) 467 at 481, H
[303] Okeke v. Nwokoye (1999) 13 NWLR (Pt.635) 495 at 509, D-E
[304] NDLEA v. Okorodudu (1997) 3 NWLR (Pt.492) 221 at 247, C
[305] Ani v. Nna (1996) 4 NWLR (Pt.440) 101 at 120, C

as having no position of his own, no policy even in the widest sense of that word."

Pius Olayiwola Aderemi, J.C.A.[306]

"Courts, being very busy institutions, cannot afford to lend their processes to be bugged or irritated by unnecessary duplications in reliefs sought. So much is on our hands and so much is to be done. We must therefore seek for the quickest way of administering justice. That will be good for all of us - the courts and the litigants."

Niki Tobi, J.C.A.[307]

"....I owe a duty not only to the administration of justice but also to the stability of the nation and the social equilibrium of the society, to point out that the frequent amendments of law, do so much harm not only to the polity but also to our existence as a people... This certainly affects the administration of justice and the victims are not only the litigants but also we the Judges and the lawyers."

Niki Tobi, J.C.A[308]

"It is the eternal credit of the courts that is the peculiar function of the Independent Judiciary comprising highly qualified legal experts burning and imbued with zeal to give final and authoritative interpretations to our constitution and our laws, that we must as far as possible, given the framework and circumstances of our times, help to nurture a society that is governed by just laws."

Ignatius Chukwudi Pats-Acholonu, J.C.A.[309]

---

[306] Anankpela v. Nigerian Army (2000) 13 NWLR (Pt.684) 224-225, E-F
[307] Akibu v. Oduntan (1992) 2 NWLR (Pt.222) 210 at 220-221, H-A
[308] Obeta v. Okpe (1996) 9 NWLR (Pt.473) 401 at 456, B-C
[309] Okoroafor v. The Miscellaneous Offences Tribunal (1995) 4 NWLR (Pt.387) 59 at 78, H

"A court of law is not a football pitch where players of the game dribble themselves with a view to winning the game by outsmarting the opponent."

Niki Tobi, J.C.A.[310]

"It is not the duty of a court or tribunal to embark upon cloistered justice by making enquiry into the case outside the open court not even by examination of documents which were in evidence but not examined in the open court. A Judge is an adjudicator; not an investigator."

Dattijo Muhammad, J.S.C[311]

---

[310] Anason Farms Ltd v. NAL Merchant Bank (1994) 3 NWLR (Pt.331) 241 at 254, A
[311] Ogboru v. Okowa (2016) 11 NWLR (Pt. 1522) 84 at 122, paras. F-G

4 CORRUPTION AND ELECTORAL MATTERS

"...the term "corrupt practices" denote or can be said to connote and embrace certain perfidious and debauched activities which are really felonious in character being redolent in their depravity and want of ethics. They become the hallmark of a decayed nature lacking in conscience and principles."

Ignatius Chukwudi Pats-Acholonu, J.S.C[312]

"The consideration for parting with the money is tainted with dirt, corruption and blatant dishonesty...It is the likes of her that watered and manured the revolting and nauseating advance fee fraud which now thrives in the mentality and culture of our society. It is a hideous culture hitherto unknown which having been introduced and allowed to flower in the minds of youths inebriated with making fast money by dishonest means has become a malignant cancer that has given this country a bad name and for which the society is fighting hard to destroy and obliterate."

Ignatius Chukwudi Pats-Acholonu, J.S.C[313]

"There are no judicial criteria or yardsticks to determine which candidate a political party ought to choose.... The question of candidate a political party will sponsor is more in the nature of a political party question which the courts are not qualified to deliberate upon and answer."

Andrews Otutu Obaseki, J.S.C[314]

"We may have to evolve any methodology in framing future Electoral Acts to make trials very short otherwise we risk having the present state of affairs coming up all the time. This would of course necessitate an amendment of the Constitution.

---

[312] Yusufu v. Obasanjo (2003) 16 NWLR (Pt.847) 554 at 641, G
[313] SBN Ltd v. De Lluch (2004) 18 NWLR (Pt.905) 341 at 358, F-H
[314] Onuoha v. R.B. Okafor & Others (1983) 2 SCNLR at 259-260

A situation where an election petition lasted more than 2 years for a 4 years presidential term leaves very much to be desired. It is an affront to the rule of law seen from an activist and progressive view point or mind."
Akintola Olufemi Ejiwunmi, J.S.C.[315]

"It now appears as a matter of general knowledge that defeated candidates in some elections are unwilling to concede defeat. They take the opportunity even on sliding stones to fight on until they drown. If some of them had the courage to acknowledge the success of their opponents, the transitional arrangements would have been clinched and the country set on the path of 'true greatness' - unity and prosperity"
Emmanuel Takon Ndoma-Egba, J.C.A.[316]

"It is scary to send policemen to election places when they have not been properly tutored that in the exercise of their duty to maintain law and order in election areas, their allegiance is to the Constitution."
Ignatius Chukwudi Pats-Acholonu, J.S.C.[317]

"Rigging or over-voting is a serious electoral malpractice. It is a most disgraceful and dishonest act that should be condemned in all its ramification, it is an illegal act."
Pius Olayiwola Aderemi, J.C.A.[318]

"There is no doubt that the manipulation and fiddling with votes reached such a gargantuan proportion that no adjudicating body in a civilized society will not state that the election should

---

[315] Buhari v. Obasanjo (2005) 13 NWLR (Pt. 941) 1 at 294, F
[316] Okoroji v. Ngwu (1992) 9 NWLR (Pt. 263) 113 at 128, D
[317] Buhari v. Obasanjo (2005) 13 NWLR (Pt. 941) 1 at 300, D
[318] Seriki v. Are (1999) 3 NWLR (Pt. 595) 469 at 480, F-G

be voided. It was a show of shame and it makes mockery of election."

Ignatius Chukwudi Pats-Acholonu, J.C.A.[319]

"A tribunal should not be swayed by alluring submissions of counsel to deprive a candidate who has cause to cry foul access to the tribunal to ventilate his grievances. It is the spurious litigant who was not a candidate who should have an up-hill task. After all, he is a busy-body, a 'meddlesome interloper', a chameleonic and unabashed impostor. Such a candidate, as described, must be looking for cheap publicity. Without shred of doubt, he must be told that he has no locus standi."

John Afolabi Fabiyi, J.C.A.[320]

"Both litigants and court will be happy with a statute which expands the frontiers of locus standi because by such expansion the doors of the court will be much more open to the litigating public and that will certainly make the rule of law and indeed democracy to triumph."

Niki Tobi, J.C.A.[321]

"…when a court declines to hear an application for injunction brought ex-parte it is engaging in a balancing process between public interest in keeping the door open for the protection of rights and the public interest in shielding judicial process from being abused."

Pius Olayiwola Aderemi, J.C.A.[322]

---

[319] Seriki v. Are (1999) 3 NWLR (Pt. 595) 469 at 481 paras E-F
[320] Nnamani v. Nnaji (1999) 7 NWLR (Pt. 610) 313 at 334 paras D-E
[321] Nnamani v. Nnaji (1999) 7 NWLR (Pt. 610) 313 at 334 paras D-E
[322] Ilori v. Benson (2000) 9 NWLR (Pt. 673) 570 at 579, G-H

"The day a court, which is also a court of justice, in the course of exercising its interpretative jurisdiction, yields or kowtows to arid legalism and abandons its primary function of doing substantial justice, a crisis situation permeates the entire system of administration of justice or the enforcement of the judicial process. Democracy in its shapeless and amorphous content and its twin brother, the rule of law, will be threatened in such a situation which will definitely result in anarchy."
Niki Tobi, J.C.A.[323]

"The silent principle in my humble opinion are the spirit of good sportsmanship to be exhibited by all the players. When an election is conducted in substantial compliance with the Act, producing a winner, other contestants should concede. This concession will strengthen our fragile strides towards democratic governance. A few concession here and there will enable electoral process on *terra firma*.

In furtherance of this principle, it is expected that where the basic requirements of an election are met, insistence upon fine details which do not constitute deliberate exclusion or infringement of the electoral law are unnecessary and could amount to frivolity."
Monica Bolna'an Dongban-Mensem, J. C. A.[324]

---

[323] Emesim v. Nwachukwu (1999) 6 NWLR (Pt.605) 154 at 169, D
[324] Agbaje v. Fashola (2008)6 NWLR (Pt.1082) 90 at 144, D-F

5 CONSTRUCTION AND INTERPRETATION

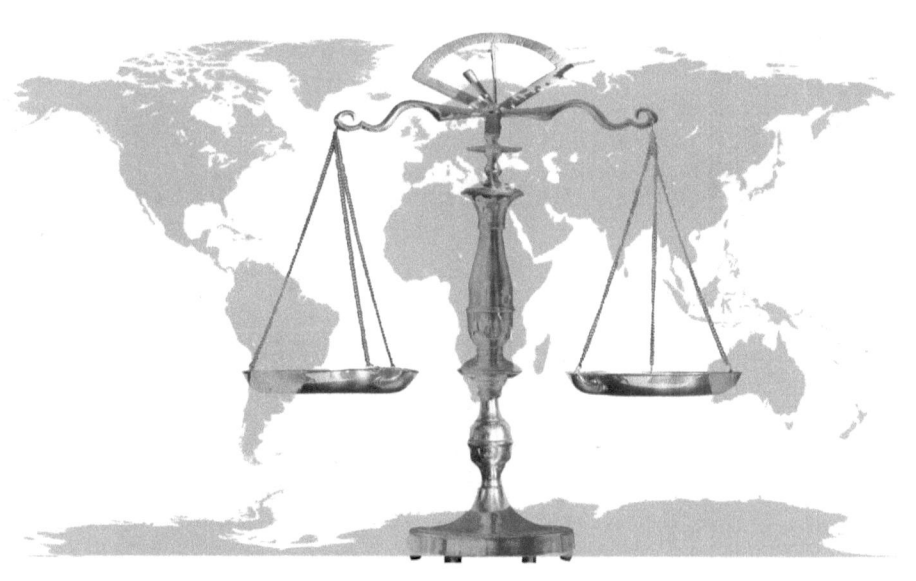

"A court indeed has no power to import into the meaning of a word something that is not in it."
Yekini Olayiwola Adio, J.S.C.[325]

"The meaning of a legislation must be collected from the plain and unambiguous expressions used rather than from any notions which may be entertained as to what is just and expedient."
Olufunlola Oyelola Adekeye, J.C.A.[326]

"It is the sacred duty of a judge to apply the law by seeking conscientiously to give fair effect to the wordings of legislative provisions. That is a duty which every judge assumes as part of the price of his independence."
Pius Olayiwola Aderemi, J.C.A.[327]

"Liberal approach to the interpretation of the Constitution is good in relevant situations, but this court cannot do excessively to the extent that it destroys the fabrics of constitutionalism and constitutionality. All interpretation of the Constitution must bow or kowtow to these twin principles or pillars of constitutional law, democracy's life blood, triumphs to the egalitarian advantage of Nigeria and its people."
Niki Tobi, J.S.C.[328]

"In modern days when good reputation is scarce commodity among mankind, possession of same by anybody is an invaluable asset which must be jealously guarded in the comity of good people. I think that is why the courts over the years have moved from liberal interpretation of those words to a seemingly strict

---

[325] Imah v. Okogbe (1993) 9 NWLR (Pt.316) 159 at 173, D-E
[326] Ararume v. INEC (2007) 9 NWLR (Pt.1038) 127 at 157, F
[327] Olatunji v. FRN (2003) 3 NWLR (Pt.807) 406 at 424, H
[328] INEC v. Musa (2003) 3 NWLR (Pt.806) 72 at 214, G-H

and hard construction. The tendency for a man to do evil is more prevalent nowadays unlike in the good old days."

Pius Olayiwola Aderemi, J.C.A.[329]

"For Law to grow the court charged with the responsibility to interpret it must strain itself to ensure that the intention of the law makers is observed. Where there is ambiguity it must give a beneficial interpretation, for ambiguity is a curse in law making and where there is curse it must be deleted from the body like a cancer."

Ignatius Chukwudi Pats-Acholonu, J.C.A.[330]

"The determination of jurisdiction is not a game of chess where there is always the chance element. Since it is not open to any guess, it is not one of the aspects of our law whether the court should use the objective or the subjective test. It is on the contrary, a matter of raw and hard law which is either donated by the constitution or by the enabling statute or by both."

Niki Tobi, J.C.A.[331]

"... the Land Use Act is not a magic wand it is being portrayed to be or a destructive monster that at once swallowed all rights on land and that the Governor or local government with mere issuance of a piece of paper, could divest families of their homes and agricultural lands overnight with a rich holder of certificate of occupancy driving them out with bulldozers and crane. The law as it is that in areas not declared urban by a state government everybody remains where he has always been as if the new Act has vested in him a customary right of occupancy."

Salihu Modibbo Alfa Belgore, J.S.C.[332]

---

[329] Access Bank Plc v. MFCCS (2005) 3 NWLR (Pt.913) 460 at 474
[330] Camptel Int'l SPA v. Dexson Ltd (1996) 7 NWLR (Pt.459) 170 at 191, B-C
[331] Afisi v. Lawal (1992) 1 NWLR (Pt.217) 350 at 366, G
[332] Ogunleye v. Oni (1990) 2 NWLR (Pt.135) 745 at 772, C-D

"The Constitution is a logical whole, each provision of which is an integral part thereof, and it is therefore logically proper and indeed imperative to construe one part in the light of the other parts."

Dennis Onyejife Edozie, J.C.A.[333]

"There is yet another important area of the principle of interpretation of our Constitution. Ours is a Nigerian Constitution, written in a Nigerian background, with a Nigerian Sociology and Nigerian experience. In the interpretation of the Constitution, Judges must have at the back of their minds the unique Nigerian nature and character of the Constitution. What this means is that a Nigerian Judge should not find himself importing a foreign decision given in a country which fundamental rights provisions are not similarly worded as ours"

Niki Tobi, J.C.A.[334]

"By its very nature a constitution must always be construed in such a way that it protects what it sets out to protect or guide what it sets out to guide."

Dalhatu Adamu, J.C.A.[335]

---

[333] Adamu v. A.G. Borno State (1996) 8 NWLR (Pt.465) 203 at 223, H quoting Kania, CJ in Gopalan v. State of Madras (1950) SCR 88 at 109
[334] Onwo v. Oko (1996) 6 NWLR (Pt.456) 584 at 613, F-G
[335] Ushae v. COP (2005) 11 NWLR (Pt.937) 499 at 524, H

6 JURISDICTION

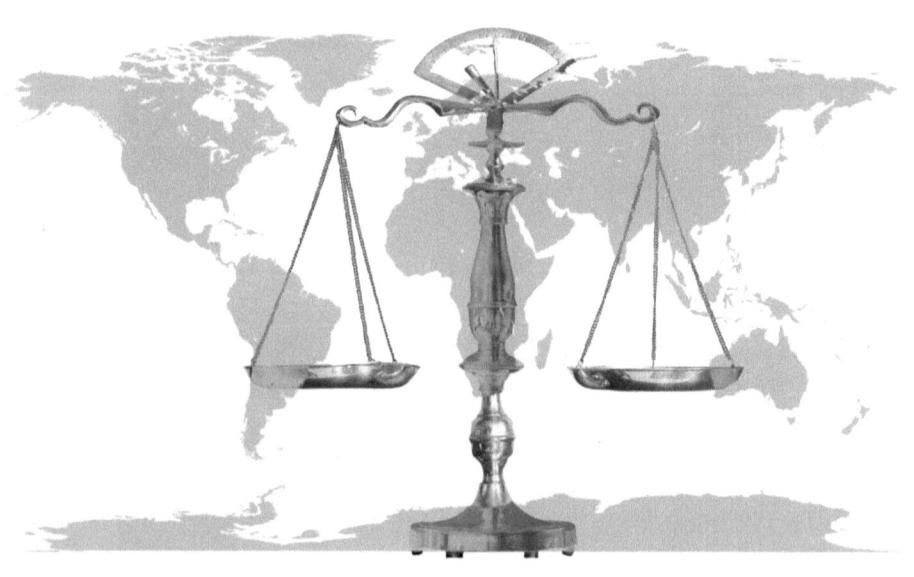

"Jurisdiction is a blood that gives life to the survival of an action in a court of law and without jurisdiction, the action will be like an animal that has been drained of its blood. It will cease to have life and any attempt to resuscitate it without infusing blood into it would be an abortive exercise."

Mohammed Bello, CJN[336]

"A court with jurisdiction builds on a solid foundation because jurisdiction is the bedrock on which court proceedings are based. But when a court lacks jurisdiction and continues to hear and determine judicial proceedings it builds on quicksand and all proceedings and steps based on it will not stand."

Ephraim Omorose Ibukun Akpata, J.S.C.[337]

"It cannot be too often repeated... that the jurisdiction of courts must be jealously guarded if only for the reason that the beginnings of dictatorship in many parts of the world had often commenced with usurpation of authority of the court and many dictators were often known to become restive under the procedural and structural safeguard employed by the courts for the purpose of enhancing the rule of law and preserving the personal and proprietary rights of individuals."

Francis Fedode Tabai, J.S.C.[338]

"It is essential in a constitutional democracy such as we have in our country, that for the protection of the rights of citizens... and for checking arbitrary use of power by the Executive or its agencies, the power and jurisdiction of the courts under

---

[336] Utih v. Onoyivwe (1991) 1NWLR (Pt.166) 166 at 206, A
[337] State v. Onagoruwa (1992) 2 NWLR (Pt.221) 33 at 58-59, H-A
[338] Adeogun v. Fashogbon (2008) 17 NWLR (Pt.1115) 149 at 175, E-G re-emphasising the decision of Aniagolu, J.S.C. in Adeyemi (Alafin of Oyo) v. A.-G., Oyo State (1984) 1 SCNLR 525 at 602, E-F

the Constitution must not only be kept intact and unfettered but also must not be nibbled at. To permit any interference with or usurpation of, the authority of the courts... is to strike at the bulwark which the Constitution gives and guarantees to the citizen, of fairness to him against all arbitrariness and oppression."
Anthony Nnaemezie Aniagolu, J.S.C.[339]

"Once a person who is aggrieved or injured by the action of another comes to court to seek redress, the court must jealously guard its jurisdiction to hear and determine the case to its finality. It cannot surrender and subject its jurisdiction to the dictates and manipulations of the defendant."
Francis Fedode Tabai, J.S.C.[340]

"To accept the argument ... that it is only the election tribunal that now has jurisdiction to hear and determine the issue of candidature of the 1st appellant at that election is to fall into a very dangerous error, or rather trap, deliberately set to ensnare the 1st respondent who was obviously not a candidate representing any political party at the said election."
Walter Samuel Nkanu Onnoghen, J.S.C.[341]

"Academic and hypothetical issues or questions do not help in the determination of the live issues in a matter. They are merely on a frolic or they are frolic-some; not touching or affecting the very tangible and material aspects in the adjudication process. As a matter of law, they add nothing to the truth searching

---

[339] Sofekun v. Akinyemi (1980) 5-7 SC 1 at 25-26
[340] Adeogun v. Fashogbon (2008) 17 NWLR (Pt.1115) 149 at 174, G-H
[341] Adeogun v. Fashogbon (2008) 17 NWLR (Pt.1115) 149 at 201, F-G

process in the administration of justice. This is because they do not relate to any relief."

Niki Tobi, J.S.C.[342]

"Any judgment which does not decide a living issue is academic and hypothetical. It stands in its best quality only as an advisory opinion. This court, and indeed any court in Nigeria, will not engage in rendering such a judgment."

Samson Odemwingie Uwaifo, J.S.C.[343]

"It is to avoid the danger of spending precious time and the Nigerian tax payers' money on proceedings which would be declared a nullity that any objection to jurisdiction must be taken at preliminary stage of the hearing. Indeed, it should be taken at the very onset of the hearing."

Sylvanus Adiewere Nsofor, J.C.A.[344]

"To avoid judicial waste of time, courts never shy away from the challenge to their jurisdiction."

Okay Achike, J.C.A.[345]

"All Judges in, whatever cadre of court they are sitting, are priests in the temple of justice. As such, Priest, they should behave in such a way as to bring respectability to the temple via the court."

Eugene Chukwuemeka Ubaezonu, J.C.A.[346]

"It is said that the decision of the Minister is administrative and not judicial. But that does not mean that he can do as he likes,

---

[342] Adeogun v. Fashogbon (2008) 17 NWLR (Pt.1115) 149 at 180, G-H
[343] A.G., Federation v. ANPP (2003) 18 (Pt.851) 182 at 215, E
[344] Adewunmi v. A.-G., Ondo State (1996) 8 NWLR (Pt.464) 73 at 91, G
[345] Ani v. Nna (1996) 4 NWLR (Pt.440) 101 at 125, H
[346] Ani v. Nna (1996) 4 NWLR (Pt.440) 101 at 127-128, H-A

regardless of right or wrong. Nor does it mean that the courts are powerless to correct him. Good administration requires that complaints should be investigated and that grievances should be remedied."

Niki Tobi, J.C.A.[347]

"A trial Judge need not wait for the case to go through the expensive process of an appeal before correcting his mistakes. Thus, once the Judge had drawn the attention of counsel on both sides to the error, omission or clerical mistake, it would be quite competent for him to correct such error, omission or mistake in the interest of justice, a Judge ought not to go on with the case when an accidental slip, a mistake or error is apparent to him."

Sylvester Umaru Onu, J.S.C.[348]

"...it is not the duty of a trial court to bridge the yawning gaps in the case presented by any of the parties."

Raphael Olufemi Rowland, J.C.A.[349]

"Dismissal of a matter in limine is to me the greatest punishment that a plaintiff can receive in the litigation process. By it the plaintiff is shut away midstream from the steam of litigation and he is in trouble. Therefore, before a trial Judge dismisses an action, he must be very sure that he has no other option open to him."

Niki Tobi, J.C.A.[350]

---

[347] Steel Bell (Nig.) Ltd v. Govt. of Cross River State (1996) 3 NWLR (Pt.438) 571 at 588, H quoting the dictum of Lord Denning in Padfield v. Minister of Agriculture Fisheries and Food (1968) AC 997
[348] Emodi v. Kwentoh (1996) 2 NWLR (Pt. 433) 656 at 681, E-F
[349] Progress Bank (Nig) Ltd v. Ugonna (Nig) Ltd (1996) 3 NWLR (Pt.435) 202 at 218, C
[350] NBCI v. MGI Co. Ltd (1992) 2 NWLR (Pt.221) 71 at 85, D

"It is always easy for the Counsel and parties to be carried away by sentiments and ubiquitous phrase interest of justice when soliciting for Courts' discretion. However, it must always be remembered that justice is meant for all parties. It is not for only one party to an action."

Suleiman Galadima, J.C.A.[351]

"The growing nature of estoppels has, however, made it difficult to appreciate its typology...From that simple origin, there has been built up over the centuries in our law, a big house with many rooms. It is the house called Estoppel. In Coke's time it was a small house with only three rooms, namely: estoppels by matter of record, by matter in writing, and by matter 'in pais'. But by our time we have so many rooms that we are apt to get confused between them."

Joseph Jeremiah Umoren, J.C.A.[352]

"Subjecting to court's jurisdiction is a serious business. Parties therefore are to be wary and cautious of consequential effects of their undertakings."

Clara Bata Ogunbiyi, J.S.C.[353]

"Court should not have the gluttony or hunger for jurisdiction in the way a child will grab sweet on its dinner table."

Niki Tobi, J.S.C.[354]

"Jurisdiction as a matter of law, and not a matter of fact, could be regularized by a plaintiff in certain circumstances. It is not

---

[351] Ntuks v. Nigerian Ports Authority (2000) 4 NWLR (Pt. 654) 639 at 650, C
[352] Atungwu v. Ochekwu (2000) 1 NWLR (Pt.641) 507 at 518C-D (quoting Lord Denning in McIlkenny v. Chief Constable of West Midlands Police Force (1980) 2 All ER 227 at 235
[353] Wema Bank Plc v. Abiodun (2006) 9 NWLR (Pt. 984) 1 at 32, H
[354] Awuse v. Odili (2003) 18 NWLR (Pt. 851) 116 at 181, E

like the facts of a case which are constant like the sun rising from the West and setting in the East every day."

Niki Tobi, J.C.A.[355]

"Time never runs against a court to decide on the issue of jurisdiction.... An attack or question as to jurisdiction cannot be properly glossed over by any court once it is raised... To do so is unwittingly to postpone the doom's day."

Okay Achike, J.S.C.[356]

"You cannot put something on nothing and expect it to stay there. It will collapse."

Isa Ayo Salami, J.C.A.[357]

---

[355] Onagoruwa v. IGP (1991) 5 NWLR (Pt. 193) 593 at 646, G
[356] Galadima v. Tambai (2000) 11 NWLR (Pt.677) 1 at 15, E, F and G
[357] Ari v. Paiko (1997) 10 NWLR (Pt.524) 335 at 356 B-C (quoting Lord Denning in Macfoy v. United Africa Company Limited (1962) AC 152 at 160

7

EVIDENCE

"There is still one aspect. It is the evidence procured under cross-examination. The cliché or aphorism that the sky is the limit of cross-examination is not good law. This is not because, (to put it lightly) the lawyer is not an astronomist or astronomer, but because there is no such law. The discipline of law is one which is characterized by limitations here and there and cross-examination cannot occupy such a tall and enviable place in our law of procedure. And here I should say that the relevancy is a limitation in all three types of examination, including cross-examination. After all, relevancy is the cynosure or heartbeat of the Law of Evidence."

Niki Tobi, J.S.C.[358]

"There is nothing magical in the use of terms like -" I believe" or "I do not believe" in appraising evidence. There is nothing esoteric in the employment of such tags. Reasons for believing or not believing a witness must be given."

John Afolabi Fabiyi, J.C.A.[359]

"To my mind, when the testimony of a witness has reached or attained the height of insipid or impotent exaggerations it should be disregarded as mere petulance and treated with ignominy."

Ignatius Chukwudi Pats-Acholonu, J.S.C.[360]

"The hallmark of a public document is its openness in that anyone can go and demand that a certified copy be given to him on paying a prescribed fee."

Tijani Abdullahi, J.C.A.[361]

---

[358] Isheno v. Julius Berger (Nig) Plc. (2008) 6 NWLR (Pt.1084) 582 at 602-603, H-B
[359] Nwosu v. Uche (2005) 17 NWLR (Pt. 955) 574 at 590, G-H
[360] C & C Const. Co. Ltd v. Okhai (2003) 18 NWLR (Pt.851) 79 at 100, E
[361] Governor of Ekiti State v. Ojo (2006) 17 NWLR (Pt.1007) 95 at 129, B

"...it is not the number of witnesses called by either side that matters as evidence is not weighed on the counting of heads but weighed by ascription of evidence of probative value derived from the testimony of the witness is what is meant in legal parlance that evidence in civil matter is based on preponderance evidence of probability."

Moronkeji Omotayo Onalaja, J.C.A.[362]

"Throughout the web of criminal law one golden thread is always to be seen, that it is the duty of the prosecution to prove the prisoner's guilt."

Uthman Mohammed, J.S.C.[363]

---

[362] Whyte v. Jack (1996) 2 NWLR (Pt.431) 407 at 441, H
[363] Onuchukwu v. State 1998) 4 NWLR (Pt.547) 576 at 592, E

8 RULES AND DISCRETION OF COURT

"...A judge is an umpire for both parties. He is not a friend to the prosecution and nor a foe to the accused. Neither vice-versa. He is after probity and credibility. Whoever wins by the weight of his evidence, is, and must be declared the successful litigant. That is why the lady carrying the scale of justice, in the justice emblem has her eyes covered or shut so that she can hand down deserved justice to a deserving litigant or party irrespective of whoever is involved."
Ibrahim Tanko Muhammad J.S.C.[364]

"Rules of court are meant to be obeyed and followed. They are not in the books for fun or as window dressing."
Olukayode Ariwoola, J.C.A.[365]

"Unless these Rules are mastered and applied properly, counsel uninitiated in the Rules and the judicial pronouncements in this regard are bound to be a disservice to the court and worst still to their clients."
Okay Achike, J.C.A.[366]

"The rules of court are to be obeyed; they are not mere rules, they are made to help the cause of justice and not to defeat justice; they are therefore aids to the court and not masters of the court..."
Muhammad Saifullahi Muntaka Coomassie, J.C.A.[367]

---

[364] Bello v. C.O.P (2018) 2 NWLR (Pt.1603) 262 at 285; 323, D-F
[365] Bayero v. Mainasara & Sons Ltd (2006) 8 NWLR (Pt.982) 391 at 423, D
[366] Onwo v. Oko (1996) 6 NWLR (Pt.456) 584 at 600, H
[367] MHWUN v. Minister of Labour & Productivity (2005) 17 NWLR (Pt.953) 120 at 147, G-H

"Rules of court must not be treated with levity and must never be sacrificed for the purpose of convenience and if it becomes necessary to compromise them, this is done to forestall injustice."
Mary Ukaego Peter-Odili, J.C.A.[368]

"Rules of court are provided to enhance the quick dispensation of cases, they are not to be manipulated and used as a vehicle for causing unnecessary delay."
Abubakar Bashir Wali, J.C.A.[369]

"Discretion does not empower a man to do what he likes because he is minded to do so. He must in the exercise of his discretion do not what he likes but what he ought…The courts do not grant a largess and the effigy of justice does not carry a cornucopia."
Aloysius Iyorgyer Katsina-Alu, J.C.A.[370]

"Courts should remain detached and no matter the appearance of the facts of the case, resist the pull of soap-opera emotion as it were and base the verdict on hard evidence."
Nwali Sylvester Ngwuta, J.S.C.[371]

---

[368] NH International SA v. NHH Limited (2007) 7 NWLR (Pt.1032) 86 at 114, G
[369] Arojoye v. UBA (1986) 2 NWLR (Pt.20) 101 at 111, H
[370] Egbuo v. Chukwu (1998) 10 NWLR (Pt.570) 499 at 510, paras. B-D
[371] Zubairu v. State (2015) 16 NWLR (Pt.1486) at 528, paras. D-F

9 EQUITY AND JUSTICE

"Definitely, law is not meant to subjugate or subvert the truth of a matter or the cause of justice".
Massaoud Abdulrahman Oredola, J.C.A.[372]

"...legal practitioners as officers in the temple of justice ought to be interested in protecting the integrity and sanctity of the administration of justice system".
Chinwe Eugenia Iyizoba J.C.A.[373]

"...Lawyers all over the world take sides for money. Though a lawyer owes a duty to the client who hires him, he must always bear in mind that he owes a higher duty to a cause higher than that of his client, the cause of justice. A lawyer who distorts or massages the facts in the record may win his client's case but such apparent victory would amount to a betrayal of justice".
Nwali Sylvester Ngwuta, J.S.C.[374]

"...Whatever the merits or otherwise of the appeal, it is a disservice to both parties and to the administration of justice for the learned counsel to engage in the type of delay tactics evident in the filing of this appeal. As an officer in the temple of justice it is the duty of learned counsel to aid and not hinder the smooth administration of justice".
Kudirat Motonmori Olatokunbo Kekere Ekun J.S.C.[375]

---

[372] Jukok Int'l v. Diamond Bank Plc. (2016) 6 NWLR (Pt.1507) 55 at 80;115, A-B
[373] J.B. Estate Development & Properties Ltd v. Nzegwu (No.2) (2016) 6 NWLR (Pt.1507) 137 at 158, A-B
[374] Bille v. State (2016) 15 NWLR (Pt.1536) 363 at 390, B-D
[375] Braithwaite v. Dalhatu (2016) 13 NWLR (Pt.1528) 32 at 57 E-G

"One principle of equity begets another principle of equity. Equity does not act in vain or in isolation. Equity must act for a purpose."

Niki Tobi, J.S.C.[376]

"Equity always incline itself to conscience, reason and good faith and it implies a system of law imposed to a just regulation of mutual rights and duties of man, in a civilized society; our own society, is not an exception to that envisaged civilized society. It does not envisage sharp practice and undue advantage of a situation and a refusal to honour reciprocal liability arising therefrom.

Pius Olayiwola Aderemi, J.C.A.[377]

"Surely equity should not be treated as a tyrannous phenomenon threatening the law. It does not exist in *vaccuo* or supposedly to roam about pouring water on the fire of the law. Equity is not a warlord determined to do battle with the law. It is a part of a legal system, which has been mixed with the law, and the admixture is for the purpose of achieving justice."

Kayode Eso, J.S.C.[378]

"...It is the monopoly of God to determine the sex of a baby and not the parents. Although the scientific world disagrees with this divine truth, I believe that God, the Creator of human being, is also the final authority of who should be male and female. Accordingly, for a custom or customary law to discriminate against a particular sex is to say the least an affront on the Almighty God Himself."

Niki Tobi, J.C.A.[379]

---

[376] Okpala v. Okpu (2003) 5 NWLR (Pt. 812) 183 at 215, H
[377] FDB Financial Services Ltd v. Adesola (2000) 8 NWLR (Pt. 668) 170 at 182, G-H
[378] Trans Bridge Co. Ltd v. Survey Inter'l Ltd (1986) 4 NWLR (Pt. 37) 576 at 598, B
[379] Mojekwu v. Mojekwu (1997) 7 NWLR (Pt.512) 283 at 305, B-C

"The rules or principles of equity help only the vigilant; they do not assist an indolent party who fails to pursue his rights diligently and within a reasonable time."
Dalhatu Adamu, J.C.A.[380]

"As courts of equity break in upon the common law, when necessity and conscience require it, still they allow superior force and strength to a legal title to estate."
Andrews Otutu Obaseki, J.S.C.[381]

"Our legal process requires a litigant to be vigilant. Once you see that your right is about to be trampled upon, you should go to court to prevent the injury or damage being done. You do not have to wait until the injury is done as the injury or damage in certain cases may be irreversible."
Eugene Chukwuemeka Ubaezonu, J.C.A.[382]

"The law, it has been said, is an ass. And the unruly ass must keep galloping along so long as Litigants refuse to follow simple rules clearly laid down in statute. This is of the very nature of justice according to law: and the courts must take the blame!"
Philip Nnaemeka-Agu, J.S.C.[383]

"This court being a court of justice is a temple of justice adhering to symbol of a blindfolded woman with a scale on one hand and a sword on the other to render "justice" (not injustice) to all manner of people. Indeed, the beauty and greatness, nay the purity of justice, in all its consuming allure and essence is to ferret out from the mass of facts and law before it relevant points in order to

---

[380] Ikpana v. RTPCN (2006) 3 NWLR (Pt. 966) 106 at 134, C-D
[381] Animashaun v. Olojo (1990) 6 NWLR (Pt. 154) 111 at 122, H
[382] A.G. Enugu State v. Omaba (1998) 1 NWLR (Pt. 532) 83 at 101, D
[383] African Petroleum Ltd v. Owodunni (1991) 8 NWLR (Pt. 210) 391 at 417, B

give remedy to anyone who comes for that. It is not justice meted to someone who does not deserve it when that person craving for it has his hand soiled, blemished and besmirched."

Ignatius Chukwudi Pats-Acholonu, J.C.A.[384]

"The delay of justice is a denial of justice. Magna Carta will have none of it. To no one will we deny or delay right of justice. All through the years men have protested at the law's delay and counted it as a grievous wrong, hard to bear. Shakespeare ranks it among the whips and scorns of time. Dickens tells how it exhausts finances, patience, courage, hope. To put right this wrong, we will in this court do all in our power to enforce expedition, and if need be, we will strike out actions when there has been excessive delay. This is a stern measure. But it is within the inherent jurisdiction of the court."

Olajide Olatawura, J.S.C.[385]

"It will smack of injustice to sacrifice justice on the altar of speedy dispensation of justice. Afterall, the justice of a case which demands that all parties before the court are given full hearing will equally frown on the uneven-handedness of the court, even if it has been prompted by the desire to dispense justice expeditiously."

Okay Achike, J.C.A.[386]

"Over-hasty proceedings, or steam rolled justice cannot be seen as true justice."

Joseph Diekola Ogundare, J.C.A.[387]

---

[384] Kwajaffa v. BON Ltd (2004) 13 NWLR (Pt.889) 146 at page 183, E-H
[385] Usikaro v. Itsekiri Land Trustees (1991) 2 NWLR (Pt.172) 150 at 180D-E quoting Lord Denning in Allen v. Alfred McAlpine & Sons Ltd (1968) 2 QB 229/245, 377
[386] Princewill v. Usman (1990) 5 NWLR (Pt.150) 274 at 283, A-B
[387] Princewill v. Usman (1990) 5 NWLR (Pt.150) 274 at 286, F-G

"Law, it must be said, cannot be wanting in dispensation of justice."
                                    Pius Olayiwola Aderemi, J.S.C.[388]

"The rules of the court...is a mere aid to administration of justice. One cannot by giving it a thwarted interpretation use it to destroy the administration of justice..."
                           Ignatius Chukwudi Pats-Acholonu, J.C.A.[389]

"The courts of this country and indeed the courts in any free society practising the tenets of democracy are established to adjudicate matters between two or more competing parties or interests. In order to facilitate and project the rule of law both in its conservative and contemporary framework, and ensure its free flow in any democratic society, parties who have submitted to the jurisdiction of the courts are bound not to take steps which are antithesis or an altercation to the accomplishments of the due process in our judicial system."
                                              Niki Tobi, J.C.A.[390]

"The flame of justice must be kept alive, be kindled and rekindled through reasoned judgments that brush aside technicalities which will be a clog in the attainment of justice."
                                        Olajide Olatawura, J.S.C.[391]

"The heyday of undue adherence to technicalities has waned and is today remembered in the doldrums of our legal history. The aim of a judicial tribunal is to strive to do justice - that is substantial justice."
                                           Okay Achike, J.C.A[392]

---

[388] Ladoja v. INEC (2007) 12 NWLR (Pt. 1017) 119 at 187, H-A
[389] Salim v. Ifenkwe (1996) 5 NWLR (Pt. 450) 564 at 588, E-F
[390] Bedding Holdings Ltd v. National Electrical Comm. (1992) 8 NWLR (Pt. 260) 428 at 437-438, H-A
[391] Egbe v. Yusuf (1992) 6 NWLR (Pt. 245) 1 at 19, E
[392] Ani v. State (1996) 5 NWLR (Pt.450) 624 at 633, A

"I do not think it is the desire of the institution of the administration of justice for counsel to criticise Judges just for the pleasure of it... I am clearly of the view that the word "inadvertence" is not complimentary to a Judges's conduct or indeed the conduct of any human being."
Niki Tobi, J.C.A.[393]

"Justice is not a one way traffic. Justice is done once it is in accordance with law. The court stands for justice for both the plaintiff and defendant in a case."
Suleiman Galadima, J.C.A.[394]

"The judicial process malfunctions and is discredited when it is bogged down by technicalities and is manipulated to go from technicality to technicality and thrive on technicalities. That is why at all times the tendency towards technicality should be eschewed and the determination to do substantial justice should remain the preferred option and hallmark of our judicial system."
Emmanuel Olayinka Ayoola, J.S.C.[395]

"I have put it on record that the desire of the judiciary to curb the now notorious attitude of some legal practitioners and politicians faced with very bad cases to employ delay tactics to either defeat the ends of justice or postpone the evil day, needs the encouragement of all well-meaning legal practitioners, particularly the very senior members of the profession....meanwhile time like tide, as they say, waits for no man; it keeps on running out and at the end may likely leave justice prostrate and the aggrieved party frustrated and bitter with the judicial system"
Walter Samuel Nkanu Onnoghen, J.S.C.[396]

---

[393] Agwuna III v. Isiadinso (1996) 5 NWLR (Pt.451) 705 at 719, B
[394] Daily Times (Nig.) Plc v. Magoro (2000) 15 NWLR (Pt.692) 855 at 867, B
[395] Maersk Line v. Addide Investment Ltd (2002) 11 NWLR (Pt.778) 317 at 383, B-C
[396] Dapianlong v. Dariye (2007) 8 NWLR (Pt.1036) 332 at 415-416, H-C

"The role of the Judge being to keep the scale of justice in the balance without tilting it to favour a party or tilting it in disfavour of the other party. It is this concept of the role of the judge that gave rise to the often quoted dictum of Chief Justice Hewart that justice should not be seen to be done but manifestly seen to have been done... Justice is rooted in confidence, once there is loss of confidence in the Judge then there is breach of fair hearing."
Moronkeji Omotayo Onalaja, J.C.A.[397]

"It has always been said that the scales of justice take snail speed. It is better to take snail speed to arrive at justice at the end of the day than to take a speed of track race and do injustice."
Niki Tobi, J.C.A.[398]

"It is important to always remind ourselves not to allow the institution for administration of justice to be used as machinery for oppression of anybody for whatever reason. If it is allowed, that will jeopardize the rule of law which is the foundation of every civilized society including Nigeria."
Walter Samuel Nkanu Onnoghen, J.C.A.[399]

"My lords, if we want to instill sanity into human affairs, if we want to entrench unpolluted democracy in our body polity, the naked truth must permeate through the blood, nerve and brain of each and every one of us. Although credit may not always have its rightful place in politics, we should try to blend the two so as to attain a fair, just and egalitarian society where no one

---

[397] Uzondu v. Uzondu (1997) 9 NWLR (Pt.521) 466 at page 483, E-F
[398] Osia v. Edjekpo (2001) 10 NWLR (Pt.720) 233 at page 248, D
[399] Akintunde v. Ojo (2002) 4 NWLR (Pt.757) 284 at page 316, H

is oppressed. Let us call a spade a spade! Let us not give a dog bad name in order to hang it."

Mahmud Muhammad, J.S.C.[400]

"The total amount in dispute is just about ₦19,387.33. I wonder how much resources had been expended by both parties in pursuing this matter in court from March 1989 to date almost 10 years. I think something is wrong somewhere. This is not one of the situations I can readily accept under the banner of development of the law…Regrettably this kind of situation lend credence to the thinking in certain quarters that our legal system is gradually becoming a lawyer's haven rather than pursuit of real justice.

Umaru Abdullahi, J.C.A.[401]

"Unnecessary intervention when uncalled for is repugnant to the ethics of the profession and dips the aura of majesty that is attendant to the position of a Judge whose mien and carriage should represent and reflect the embodiment of justice cast in the mould of a female that is blindfolded and firmly holding the scale of justice in one hand and sword on the other"

Ignatius Chukwudi Pats-Acholonu, J.C.A.[402]

"The vigilant and not the sleeping litigant is the one who is assisted by the laws. This is so because the law always abhors delay. The time honoured aphorism is that justice delayed is said to be justice denied."

Pius Olayiwola Aderemi, J.C.A.[403]

---

[400] Ugwu v. Ararume (2007) 12 NWLR (Pt.1048) 367 at page 514, D-E
[401] UBN Ltd v. Ayoola (1998) 11 NWLR (Pt.573) 338 at 343, G-H
[402] Elias v. Elias (2001) 9 NWLR (Pt.718) 429 at pages 445-446, H-A
[403] Wellington v. Regd. Trustees, Ijebu-Ode (2000) 3 NWLR (Pt.647) 130 at 139, D-E

"Technicality in the administration of justice shuts out justice. A litigant sent out of court without a hearing is denied justice. A man denied on any ground much less a technical ground grudges the administration of justice. It is therefore better to have a case heard and determined on merits than to leave the court with a shield of 'victory' obtained on mere technicalities."

Olajide Olatawura, J.S.C.[404]

"...ignorance of the law is no excuse: *ignorantia juris non excusat*. It is therefore a true rule that every man must be taken to be cognizant of the law; for otherwise there is no saying to what extent the excuse of ignorance might not be carried: it would be urged in almost every case."

Owolabi Kolawole, J.C.A.[405]

"The day a party who has not committed a wrong is made to suffer a reverse or victimized in the judicial process by way of such sanction, the judicial system should receive a censor from the public. How this will be carried out I am not prepared to theorize here. I leave that for a most appropriate situation."

Niki Tobi, J.C.A.[406]

"The court is the citizen's bulwark against the invasion of liberty."

George Adesola Oguntade, J.C.A.[407]

"It is a cardinal principle of the administration of justice to let a party know the fate of his application whether properly or improperly brought before the court. It will amount to unfair

---

[404] Nipol Ltd v. Bioku Invest. & Property Co. Ltd (1992) 3 NWLR (Pt.232) 727 at 753, D-E
[405] Chrisray (Nig) Ltd v. Elson & Neil Ltd (1990) 3 NWLR (Pt.140) 630 at 641, G
[406] Emesim v. Nwachukwu (1999) 6 NWLR (Pt.605) 154 at 169, E
[407] Compt. Nig. Prison Service v. Adekanye (1999) 6 NWLR (Pt. 607) 381 at 388, G-H

hearing to ignore an objection raised by a party or his counsel against any step in the proceedings."
Uthman Mohammed, J.S.C.[408]

"Right must be correlated with duty. It is not enough to parade a fellow citizen before the court in delirium of ecstasy with the full authority of the State on a vacuous accusation of capital offence."
Sule Aremu Olagunju, J.C.A.[409]

"The courts are duty bound to see that cases are speedily determined. In fact, it is a denial of justice to keep a matter for too long without trial. Justice delayed is justice denied."
Rabiu Danlami Muhammad, J.C.A.[410]

"It is not the duty of the court to do cloistered justice by making an enquiry into the case outside the court…"
Mohammed Bello, C.J.N.[411]

"No matter the delay, if dispensation of justice is the ultimate end, then that delay is worth it. Justice must never be seen to be slaughtered on the altar of speed."
Pius Olayiwola Aderemi, J.C.A.[412]

"The term 'public policy' is in my view not only an unruly horse but a double edged sword. It is against public policy to enforce an illegal contract in Nigeria. It will also be against public policy

---

[408] Onyekwuluje v. Animashaun (1996) 3 NWLR (Pt. 439) 637 at 644, G-H
[409] Ejimkonye v. State (2000) 3 NWLR (Pt.648) 262 at 273, E-F
[410] Waniko v. Ade-John (1999) 8 NWLR (Pt.619) 401 at 410, C-D
[411] Onibudo v. Akibu (1982) 7 SC 60 at 62
[412] Equity Bank (Nig.) Ltd v. Daura (1999) 10 NWLR (Pt.621) 147 at 159, E

to allow a debtor to get away with his obligation under the fruits of a valid judgment."
Atinuke Omobonike Ige, J.C.A.[413]

"This court is not a mechanical and automatic calculator. No. it is a court of law dealing with varying situations and applying the same law to these situations in order to do justice in each and every situation according to its peculiar surrounding circumstances."
Chukwudifu Akunne Oputa, J.S.C.[414]

"...where technicality touches a fundamental objective to fair hearing, it cannot be ignored."
Uthman Mohammed, J.S.C.[415]

"Justice can only be done if the substance of the matter is examined. Reliance on technicalities leads to injustice."
Raphael Olufemi Rowland, J.C.A.[416]

"Courts in all civilized societies are averse to sticking strictly to the words of the statute so as not to appear to be dogmatic, in not relenting to give a citizen whose freedom is in jeopardy a chance to get off if that is possible."
Ignatius Chukwudi Pats-Acholonu, J.C.A.[417]

"Justice is said to be rooted in confidence. That confidence will be lost if an ordinary but a reasonable man who enters into the citadel of justice to watch the proceedings ...can reasonably

---

[413] Macaulay v. RZB of Austria (1999) 4 NWLR (Pt. 600) 599 at 611-612, H-A
[414] Ohuka v. State (1988) 1 NWLR (Pt.72) 539 at 550, B
[415] Onyekwuluje v. Animashaun (1996) 3 NWLR (Pt.439) 637 at 644, G
[416] Chevron (Nig.) Ltd v. Onwugbelu (1996) 3 NWLR (Pt.437) 404 at 419D quoting the Supreme Court in The State v. Gwanto (1983) 3 SC 62 at 76
[417] Amadi v. Military Administrator of Imo State (2000) 4 NWLR (Pt.652) 328 at 337, C

reach a conclusion that the judex is biased by his comments or observations"

Pius Olayiwola Aderemi, J.C.A.[418]

"I do not see that a judge's mind will not be stirred against the situation where some persons who are yet to be tried for offences have been put in custody for over three years. How do you compensate such persons if they are eventually found not guilty? It is a sad and unfortunate situation. To put it mildly, no civilized system ought to permit this situation."

George Adesola Oguntade, J.C.A.[419]

"Where an issue affects the props, foundations and fundamentals of a case, a court of law is not competent to hide under the rule against technicalities and ignore it. While a court of law thinks it takes that line of action in vindication of justice, the reality is that it is doing grave injustice to justice. I say so because the moment an issue affects the merits of the entire case and it is put under the carpet as being technical, the party in favour of which the issue arises is denied justice as he returns home from the court with injustice."

Niki Tobi, J.C.A.[420]

"It is often said that 'Justice delayed is justice denied'. The corollary of this is 'hush-hush justice'."

Raphael Olufemi Rowland, J.C.A.[421]

---

[418] Hayes v. Hayes (2000) 3 NWLR (Pt.648) 276 at 294, G-H
[419] Compt. Nig. Prison Service v. Adekanye (1999) 6 NWLR (Pt.607) 381 at 388, G-H
[420] Adeniji v. State (1992) 4 NWLR (Pt.234) 248 at 265, H-A
[421] Chevron (Nig.) Ltd v. Onwugbelu (1996) 3 NWLR (Pt.437) 404 at 419, G

"People in the area of justice should collectively have a second hard look at our legal system."
Umaru Abdullahi, J.C.A.[422]

"In our system of criminal adjudication, the Judge has to hold the balance between the prosecution and the defence. To do anything which gives advantage to the prosecution is to tilt the balance of justice rather fatally."
Kayode Eso, J.S.C.[423]

"The principle of fair hearing or fair trial, as it is also called, is a large and gigantic term which is provided for, not only in the constitution of the land, but also at common law as adumbrated in the two twin rules of natural justice. They are the principles, of *audi alteram partem* and *nemo judex in causa sua*. And because of the omnibus content of the principle, counsel resort to it regularly and in quite a number of instances or situations, receive remedy."
Niki Tobi, J.C.A.[424]

"A learned person known as Ustaz Mamman drew attention of the appellant and his co-accused persons that they had no authority to take away the life of the deceased, yet they kept deaf ears and even described, Ustaz as an infidel. I cannot see how these kinds of people shall have respite by the law. What is good for the goose is good for the gander: Life is precious to all and sundry. He who kills by the sword shall die by the sword. I have no sympathy for the banishment of such busy bodies who respect no human life due to their high degree of

---
[422] UBN Ltd v. Ayoola (1998) 11 NWLR (Pt.573) 338 at 343, H
[423] Akinfe v. The State (1988) 3 NWLR (Pt.85) 729 at 754, D
[424] Okeke v. Nwokoye (1999) 13 NWLR (Pt. 635) 495 at 508, C-D

misapprehension of the law or; should I say, complete ignorance of the law."
Ibrahim Tanko Muhammad, J.S.C.[425]

"Let it be said that it is especially important for the healthy development of our criminal jurisprudence that there is the assurance that the doors that may lead to the truth remain unlocked to all parties."
Pius Olayiwola Aderemi, J.C.A.[426]

"And justice is not a one-way traffic. It is not justice for the appellant only. Justice is not even only a two-way traffic. It is really a three-way traffic-justice for the appellant accused of a heinous crime of murder; justice for the victim, the murdered man, the deceased, "whose blood is crying to heaven for vengeance" and finally justice for the society at large - the society whose social norms and values had been desecrated and broken by the criminal act complained of..."
Chukwudifu Akunne Oputa, J.S.C.[427]

"The Judge however wise, creative and imaginative he may be, is combined, cribbed, confined, bound in, not as Macbeth to his saucy doubts and fears but by evidence and arguments of litigants. It is this limitation inherent in the forensic process, which sets bounds to the scope of judicial law."
Niki Tobi, J.C.A.[428]

"Judges are so desirous of being fair that they loath to curtail forensic opportunities. We do not worship at the shrine of

---

[425] Shalla v. State (2007) 18 NWLR (Pt.1066) 240 at pages 299, C-D
[426] Anyankpele v. Nigerian Army (2000) 13 NWLR (Pt.684) 209 at 222, D
[427] Josiah v. The State (1985) 1 NWLR (Pt.1) 125 at 141, G-H
[428] Nwagbogu v. Abadom (1994) 7 NWLR (Pt.356) 357 at 376-377 H-A quoting Lord Scarman in Choo v. Canden Islington Area Health Authority (1979) 2 All E.R. 910

formalism; we do not follow the false gods which are satisfied by oblation and ceremonies. We are free citizens of a republic with an unprecedented opportunity for an orderly progress and for an ever wider diffusion of prosperity which are impossible save as justice is adequately served..."

Ignatius Chukwudi Pats-Acholonu, J.C.A.[429]

"A wrong or illegal foot-setting or a wrong and bad foundation would result in a wobble building and if the wrong footing involves a condition precedent to the assumption of jurisdiction, all other acts performed upon such a wrong and wobble jurisdiction will fail like a pack of cards. A house built on a wobble foundation cannot stand."

Ibrahim Kolapo Sulu-Gambari, J.C.A.[430]

"Justice is justice if only it attains the basic tenets of the litigation before the court. Justice is aimed at ensuring that the parties in the litigation are fairly treated or receive a fair deal from the court without any element of bias."

Niki Tobi, J.C.A.[431]

"The Judges seek the truth so as to know the justice of a case. They apply the law to the facts in order to attain justice. In an attempt to do all or any of these, the courts sometimes err in law or misdirect themselves. These mistakes and error are thereafter corrected by appellate courts. If the road to justice is plain and smooth, there will hardly be any case for appellate courts... Consequently, it takes time to know the truth of a case... The

---

[429] Okoroafor v. The Miscellaneous Offences Tribunal (1995) 4 NWLR (Pt. 387) 59 at 78, C quoting Hon. Justice Charles Hughes in an address delivered to American Bar Association published in ABA Journal, Sept. 1925
[430] Okoroafor v. The Miscellaneous Offences Tribunal (1995) 4 NWLR (Pt.387) 59 at 81, H
[431] Carribbean Trading & Fidelity Corp. v. NNPC (1992) 7 NWLR (Pt.252) 161 at 182, H

long time spent before justice is done is better than the harm done in a shorter period and perpetuated forever. We should not sacrifice justice for speedy trial."

Olajide Olatawura, J.S.C.[432]

"We no longer insist upon the old rule that only the opinion of the illustrious dead could rule the living in our courts. If a contemporary jurist puts forward a convincing proposition on a recondite point of law on which there is no decided authority there is now nothing wrong with a court accepting and applying it, particularly in the top echelon of our judicial hierarchy."

Philip Nnaemeka-Agu, J.S.C.[433]

"Courts are wont to construe provisions in the statute in a manner that would be beneficial to the over-all interest of the society and tend to view with askance any tendency to a construction that would not stand the test of justice or which may be regarded as an affront to reason, decency and decorum."

Ignatius Chukwudi Pats-Acholonu, J.C.A.[434]

The judge is to keep off the arena if he does not want his view to be blurred by the dust rising therefrom. For that reason, the judge is not to descend into the arena."

Isa Ayo Salami, J.C.A.[435]

"A Judge may be genuinely anxious to deal with a matter expeditiously with a view to clearing his long and heavy cause list, and in the process run foul against the rules of court. That does not, in my humble view, make the Judge lack "the

---

[432] Oshoboja v. Amuda (1992) 6 NWLR (Pt.250) 690 at 709, F-G
[433] Osafile v. Odi (No.1) (1990) 3 NWLR (Pt.137) 130 at 155, C-D
[434] Okoroafor v. The Miscellaneous Offences Tribunal (1995) 4 NWLR (Pt.387) 59 at 75, H-A
[435] Amogun v. Adesina (1994) 4 NWLR (Pt.339) 503 at 509, H

desirability of remaining an impartial arbiter between the parties."

Niki Tobi, J.C.A.[436]

"...it is not the function of a trial Judge by his own exercise or ingenuity to supply or imagine evidence or to work out the mechanics or mathematics of arriving at answers which only evidence tested under cross-examination can apply."

Anthony Ikechukwu Iguh, J.S.C.[437]

"While it is obligatory on the courts to give meaning to the provisions of the fundamental human rights entrenched in our Constitution, the court must balance it against the equally compelling demand for public justice."

Emmanuel Obioma Ogwuegbu, J.S.C.[438]

"Pleadings have no mouth to talk in Court. They therefore remain docile in the case file until life is given to them by a witness who leads evidence on them. It is only then that the court takes cognizance of them by attaching or apportioning evidential weight as necessary."

Niki Tobi, J.C.A.[439]

"It is the duty of the court to nurture, preserve and even expand the horizons of law with the ultimate intention to make access to the courts a reality. When free and unfettered access to justice is jeopardized in whatever form, but more particularly

---

[436] Orakwute v. Agagwu (1996) 8 NWLR (Pt.466) 359 at 375, G
[437] Princewill v. State (1994) 6 NWLR (Pt.353) 703 at 715, C
[438] Effiom v. State (1995) 1 NWLR (Pt.373) 507 at 617, C
[439] NITEL Plc v. Rockonoh Property Co. Ltd (1995) 2 NWLR (Pt. 378) 473 at 496, G-H

by questionable judicial pronouncement, then it is time to act fast and save the situation."
Ignatius Chukwudi Pats- Acholonu, J.C.A.[440]

"A speculative or conjectural charge of bias on the part of a Judge is not only unfair to the exalted position of the Judge *qua judem*, but also to the entire administration of justice system in which learned counsel also plays a leading role."
Niki Tobi, J.C.A.[441]

"The fundamental duty of any court or any tribunal entrusted with dispensation of justice is to do justice or substantial justice to both parties to the litigation. Judicial activism in my view does not mean judicial recklessness such that may lead to chaos, nor does it mean bending the law in favour of one side to the detriment of the other."
Abubakar Bashir Wali, J.S.C.[442]

"...courts of law, being the custodian of justice, will not lend the machinery of justice to do injustice."
Niki Tobi, J.C.A.[443]

"A situation where the court literally took over the examination in chief or cross examination of a witness may compel a party's counsel to sit down. And, when the trial Judge has finished asking series of questions and the counsel continues to sit down and when the court asks him to continue could draw a remark

---

[440] Houtmangracht v. Oduba (1995) 1 NWLR (Pt.371) 295 at 311, D
[441] Orakwute v. Agagwu (1996) 8 NWLR (Pt.466) 359 at 375, H
[442] Effiom v. State (1995) 1 NWLR (Pt.373) 507 at 585, C-D
[443] NITEL Plc v. Rockonoh Property Co. Ltd (1995) 2 NWLR (Pt.378) 473 at 512, A

of "Oh yes my Lord, but I am waiting for your Lordship to call your next witness."
Ignatius Chukwudi Pats-Acholonu, J.C.A.[444]

"A trial court... has no jurisdiction to go out on a voyage of its own in search of greener pastures or softer terrain for one of the parties, in the guise of doing justice. By such action, the court has derailed from its constitutional, statutory and common law role of impartial adjudication of the issue or issues before it. That is not justice."
Niki Tobi, J.C.A.[445]

"The aim of the courts, for quite a long time now, has been to do substantial justice between the parties. The days of technicality or technical justice have gone forever."
Bode Rhodes-Vivour, J.C.A.[446]

"I would wish to underscore the fact that the adversary system of administration of justice which we operate has no room for any sneak game of hide and seek."
Philip Nnaemeka-Agu, J.S.C.[447]

"Such garrulity or needless excitement which makes a Judge descend into the arena of trial as though he is a party offends an ethical behavior expected of a Judge and must be avoided as it may upset the delicate balance of the case."
Ignatius Chukwudi Pats-Acholonu, J.C.A.[448]

---

[444] Ibrahim v. State (1995) 3 NWLR (Pt.381) 35 at 48, E-F
[445] NITEL Plc v. Rockonoh Property Co. Ltd. (1995) 2 NWLR (Pt.378) 473 at 512, A
[446] NIC v. Acen Insurance Co. Ltd & 92 Ors (2007) 6 NWLR (Pt.1031) 589 at 600, F
[447] Agbonifo v. Aiwereoba (1988) 1 NWLR (Pt.70) 325 at 342, H
[448] Ibrahim v. State (1995) 3 NWLR (Pt.381) 35 at 48, F-G

"The spirit of justice does not reside in formalities or words, nor is the triumph of its administration to be found in successfully picking a way between the pitfalls of technicality. After all, the law is, or ought to be but the handmaid of Justice, and flexibility, which is the most becoming robe of (law), often serves to render (justice) grotesque."
Ibrahim Tanko Muhammad, J.C.A.[449]

"...a court of law deals with substantial justice, equity and fair play and frowns at academic issues."
Moronkeji Omotayo Onalaja, J.C.A.[450]

"Justice must be even handed. A judgment which is more concerned with the interest of one party alone is obviously bereft of any rational basis and is not reflective of the nature of our judicial system.
Ignatius Chukwudi Pats- Acholonu, J.C.A.[451]

"...a court of law should not only temper justice with mercy but what is sometimes vitally important, it should also temper mercy with justice."
Chukwudifu Akunne Oputa, J.S.C.[452]

"...where there is no basis for the finding or believe of a trial court and once such finding is made it becomes perverse and substantial miscarriage of justice is bound to occur."
Aloma Mariam Mukhtar, J.C.A.[453]

---

[449] Salami v. Bunginimi (1998) 9 NWLR (Pt.565) 235 at 243 quoting Lord Penzance in Combe v. Edwards (1878) LR 34 PD 103 at 142
[450] Pelfaco Ltd v. W.A.O.S. Ltd (1997) 10 NWLR (Pt.524) 222 at 238, F
[451] Houtmangracht v. Oduba (1995) 1 NWLR (Pt.371) 295 at 311, B-C
[452] Kajubo v. State (1988) 1 NWLR (Pt.73)721 at 738, G
[453] Folarin v. State (1995) 1 NWLR (Pt.371) 313 at 323, C

"It does great disservice to the administration of justice and to public respect for the law, when a guilty man escapes punishment."
Dauda Azaki, J.C.A.[454]

"A state of affairs in which this country's image of justice may be pilloried because of the stand of a court which makes horrendous orders that will frighten foreign companies that deal with our country in business matters must necessarily be scorched."
Ignatius Chukwudi Pats- Acholonu, J.C.A.[455]

"A demand for a speedy trial, which has no regard to the conditions and circumstances in this country, will be unrealistic and be worse than unreasonable delay in trial itself."
Yekini Olayiwola Adio, J.S.C.[456]

"In my view, if there are two routes to the truth searching or truth finding process and one of the routes is shorter than the other, a trial court is well advised to follow the shorter route, if it will result in doing the same justice to the parties, as the longer route. This will certainly save the already crowded time of the court and it will help in no little way in the quick dispensation of justice. The court will like it. The parties will like it too.
Niki Tobi, J.C.A.[457]

"…the age-long principle of law, that law and morality are almost always poles apart, is still very much alive."
Ibrahim Tanko Muhammad, J.C.A.[458]

---

[454] Folarin v. State (1995) 1 NWLR (Pt.371) 313 at 323, F-G quoting Brett, F.J. in LatifuGbadamosi v. Queen (1959) 4 FSC 181 at 183
[455] Houtmangracht v. Oduba (1995) 1 NWLR (Pt.371) 295 at 311, E
[456] Effiom v State (1995) 1 NWLR (Pt.373) 507 at 622, C
[457] Okpokpo v. Uko (1997) 11 NWLR (Pt.527) 114 at 125, F-G
[458] P.A.N. v. Oje (1997) 11 NWLR (Pt.530) 625 at 636, C-D

"Instances may exist where short cut may prove invaluable and achieve their objectives. It is, however, generally to be recognized that in legal matters and particularly in matters of natural justice, short circuiting legal norms and norms of natural justice could end in rendering the whole exercise a futility. In that case, the short cut becomes the ineffective longer route."

Anthony Nnaemezie Aniagolu, J.S.C.[459]

"A state is not a knight in shining armour undertaking the errands of just any of its citizens around. If it does, it may turn itself into the legendary Don Quixote who strikes at imaginary windmills."

Kayode Eso, J.S.C[460]

"We must balance the need not to delay justice with an important requisite of justice - non-denial of justice by not refusing adjournment where compensation by way of costs will be adequate and just. Delayed justice is bad, but denial of justice is worse and outrageous. The denial inflicts pain, grief, suffering and untold hardship on those who rely on impartial administration of justice."

Olajide Olatawura, J.S.C.[461]

"I believe that law and justice should at all times be the mirror by which the society gauges how administration of justice devoid of all technicalities, or reliance on old hackneyed disputable mumbo expressions, is readily understandable and appreciated by a person in the street."

Ignatius Chukwudi Pats-Achonolu, J.S.C.[462]

---

[459] State Civil Service Commission v. Alexius I. Buzugbe (1984) 7 SC 19
[460] AG Ondo State v. AG Federation and 19 Ors (1983) 2 SCNLR 269 at 277
[461] Ceekay Traders v. General Motors Co. Ltd. (1992) 2 NWLR (Pt.222)132 at 162, D
[462] Adava v. State (2006) 9 NWLR (Pt.984) 152 at 178, H (Dissenting Opinion)

"It caricatures the entire concept of legality and of a legal right to say that violation of a law or of a legal right becomes an academic question and ceases to be actionable if and when the violation stops..."

Niki Tobi, J.S.C.[463]

"Justice and all that it connotes is a very serious business and should not be seen to be toyed with lightly."

Amina Adamu Augie, J.C.A.[464]

"It is my belief and I hold dearly to it that when law and justice are subjected to abstract reasoning or reduced to mere fantasies that they are removed from the realm of realities, then the growth of jurisprudence is stunted and we may unwittingly use old, worn out and outmoded methods, cliché and illogicality to confront a problem of the present time."

Ignatius Chukwudi Pats-Acholonu, J.S.C.[465]

"A party who commits a wrongful act cannot benefit from the self same act."

Francis Fedode Tabai, J.C.A.[466]

"It is in the interest of the best administration of justice that where the issue of jurisdiction is raised in any proceedings before any court of law, it should be dealt with at the earliest opportunity and before trial or consideration of any other issues raised in the case, as anything done without or in excess of

---

[463] Plateau State v. A.G. Federation (2006) 3 NWLR (Pt.967) 346 at 420, D
[464] SPD (Nig.) Ltd v. Arho-Joe (Nig.) Ltd. (2006) 3 NWLR (Pt.966) 172 at 193, A
[465] Adava v. State (2006) 9 NWLR (Pt.984) 152 at 177, F-G
[466] Akanni v. Olaniyan (2006) 8 NWLR (Pt.983) 531 at 546, B

jurisdiction by any court established under the Constitution is a nullity."

Mahmud Mohammed, J.C.A.[467]

"The theory of justice to which we adhere rests apriori on the premise that there must be certainty and parties to the legal duel should be in a position to know where they stand at a certain time.

Ignatius Chukwudi Pats-Acholonu, J.C.A.[468]

"It beats me hollow for any thought that a procedure which ably gives room for the doing of justice is referred to as technical. What then is justice? Justice is never built on technicalities but on what is just and fair in any given situation. A procedure which is built on justice cannot be regarded as technical.

Niki Tobi, J.S.C.[469]

"It is lame argument to say that private individuals or persons do not corrupt officials or get them to abuse their power. It is good sense that everyone involved in corrupt practices and abuse of power should be made to face the law in our effort to eradicate this cankerworm."

Aloysius Iyorgyer Katsina-Alu, J.S.C.[470]

"Of all forms of tyranny, it appears beyond question that the judicial kind is the most total and awesome. Once the Judge, the court that is, is tyrannical in the delivery of its services, the consumers of such services are without further remedy to a gruesome abuse."

Musa Dattijo Muhammad, J.C.A.[471]

---

[467] Odessa v. FRN (No.2) (2005) 10 NWLR (Pt.934) 518 at 559, A-C
[468] Peters v. Ashamu (1995) 4 NWLR (Pt.388) 206 at 222, B
[469] Okpala v. Okpu (2003) 5 NWLR (Pt.812) 183 at 214, H
[470] AG Ondo State v. AG Federation (2002) 9 NWLR (Pt.772) 222 at 364, G-H
[471] Moghalu v. Ngige (2005) 4 NWLR (Pt.914) 1 at 32, E-F

"There is no wisdom in pursuing a legal right with raw bravado employing crude extra-judicial measure that has the tendency of impairing the object of the right, albeit unwittingly."
Sule Aremu Olagunju, J.C.A.[472]

"Justice is much more than a game of hide and seek. It is an attempt, our human imperfections notwithstanding, to discover the truth. Justice will never decree anything in favour of a slippery party."
Chukwudifu Akunne Oputa, J.S.C.[473]

"Courts of law should draw a dichotomy or cleavage between our adjectival laws which are based on fundamental rules of natural justice and those which are based on mere technicalities and therefore pursue the shadow of the litigation rather than the substance of it."
Niki Tobi, J.S.C.[474]

"A Tribunal or court of law is neither a laboratory nor a scientific workshop of handwriting experts where technology is available to analyse handwriting... A Tribunal is just an institution established for the determination of legal dispute between two or more persons."
Niki Tobi, J.C.A.[475]

"I do not conceive it to be the duty of this court so to construe any of the provisions of the constitution as to defeat the obvious ends the constitution was designed to serve where another construction equally in accord and consistent with the words

---

[472] UTB Ltd v. Dol. Pharm. (Nig.) Ltd (2002) 8 NWLR (Pt.770) 726 at 751, E
[473] Ajide v. Kelani (1985) 3 NWLR (Pt.12) 248 at 269, D
[474] Okpala v. Okpu (2003) 5 NWLR (Pt.812) 183 at 214, G-H
[475] Zimit v. Mahmoud (1993) 1 NWLR (Pt.267) 71 at 90, E

and sense of such provisions will serve to enforce and protect such ends."

Michael Ekundayo Ogundare, J.C.A.[476]

"A Judge is the master of his court. It is his primary duty to control proceedings in his court in such a way that there should be no breach or contravention of the accepted procedure for hearing and disposing of a case before him."

Eugene Chukwuemeka Ubaezonu, J.C.A.[477]

"It is the duty of courts to do substantial justice by correctly interpreting our legislation without regard to possible reaction of the executive arms of the government. To attempt to anticipate government on the issue tantamounts to speculation and courts are not given to speculations."

Isa Ayo Salami, J.C.A.[478]

"The court, no matter how vigilant or generous, cannot by its overzealousness or fastidiousness, surreptitiously steal, as it were, the legal battle from the combatants (i.e. the parties) by arbitrarily imposing proof of matters not within the contemplation of the case already made out by the parties."

Okay Achike, J.C.A.[479]

"The judge, however wise, creative and imaginative he may be, is 'cabin'd, crib'd, confin'd, bound in' not as Macbeth to his

---

[476] Okhae v. Governor, Bendel State (1990) 4 NWLR (Pt.144) 327 at 356D quoting Sir Udoma, J.S.C. in Rabiu v. The State (1980) 8-11 SC 130 at 148-149
[477] Oteju v. Oluguna (1992) 8 NWLR (Pt.262) 752 at 770, C
[478] Okulaja v. Adefulu (1992) 5 NWLR (Pt.244) 752 at 766, F-G
[479] Hayaki v. Dogara (1993) 8 NWLR (Pt.313) 586 at 598, G

'fancy doubts and fears' but by the evidence and arguments of the litigants."
George Adesola Oguntade, J.C.A.[480]

"The justification for the doctrine of judicial precedent is that it ensures some amount of certainty in the law. That does not conceive of its application to stultify the law or make it a mechanical or unimaginative concept. This means that a judicial authority must be applied in relation to the facts of a case."
Samson Odemwingie Uwaifo, J.C.A.[481]

".... inherent jurisdiction or power is a necessary adjunct of the powers conferred by the Rules and is invoked by a court of law to ensure that the machinery of justice is duly applied and properly lubricated."
Philip Nnaemeka-Agu, J.S.C.[482]

"A Tribunal or Court of Law cannot embark on a voyage of discovery; a voyage which is characterized by unsafe speculations and conjectures. After all, it is not Christopher Columbus. A Tribunal which embarks upon an unguarded voyage of discovery will be lost in the sea and cannot swim or float ashore. That will be bad, not only for the judicial institution, but also for the litigants, since there will be no such institution to adjudicate on competing interests of parties."
Niki Tobi, J.C.A.[483]

"If we must practice democracy at the stage and on the platform of due process and the rule of law, we must learn to know the

---
[480] Ndiwe v. Shingleton& Co. Ltd (1993) 2 NWLR (Pt. 274) 242 at 250, D-E quoting Eso, J.S.C. who quoted Lord Scarman in Sodipo v. Lemminkainen OY (No.1) (1986) 1 S.C. 197 at 217
[481] Iwuno v. Dieli (1990) 5 NWLR (Pt.149) 126 at 134, H
[482] Arubo v. Aiyeleru (1993) 3 NWLR (Pt.280) 126 at 142, A
[483] Zimit v. Mahmoud (1993) 1 NWLR (Pt.267) 71 at 91, E-F

limits of our powers and acknowledge the extent of the powers of others. The first lesson is that institutions which ensure democracy must not be allowed to take any other form and be personalized. If they are, they become open to grave abuse."

Samson Odemwingie Uwaifo, J.C.A.[484]

"Every Judge in Nigeria has sworn to do justice according to law. The laws to be applied by a court in all cases are not limited to only those authorities, statutory and judicial, which have been cited for the court's consideration by counsel on both sides. Rather, they include those laws which the court can judicially notice as well as those relevant to the issue before the court which the court can from its own research find out. If Judges do otherwise they will be deciding contrary to laws which they have sworn to uphold."

Philip Nnaemeka-Agu, J.S.C.[485]

"The Constitution is the highest law of the land. All other laws bow or kowtow to it for 'salvation'. No law which is inconsistent with it will survive. That law must die and for the good of the society."

Niki Tobi, J.C.A.[486]

"It seems clear that (the Participation in Politics and Elections (Prohibitions) Act, 1987) was a bold attempt to purify the political practice in this country by ferreting therefrom corrupt and dishonest persons. No one who is familiar with the history of this country and the harm done to her in the past by corrupt and dishonest practices can fail to appreciate the desirability of

---

[484] Bamidele v. Commissioner for Local Govt & Community Dev., Lagos State (1994) 2 NWLR (Pt.328) 568 at 586, D
[485] Finnih v. Imade (1992) 1 NWLR (Pt.219) 511 at 542, C-D
[486] Phoenix Motors Ltd v. N.P.F.M.B. (1993) 1 NWLR (Pt.272) 718 at 730, C

keeping political aculture and practices as clean as possible in our fresh attempt at democratic governance."
> **George Adesola Oguntade, J.C.A.**[487]

"...the courts tend to be flexible in respect of procedural law as the end of justice is to do real justice, rules of court may at times be juggled now and then to meet the ends of justice as they are mere aids to the court in its quest for justice."
> **Ignatius Chukwudi Pats-Acholonu, J.S.C.**[488]

"As a matter of general principles of avoiding injustice and absurdity, a court would not allow a person to profit by his own wrong. A person may not create a crisis situation and turn around to plead the crisis in support of his interest."
> **Anthony Nnaemezie Aniagolu, J.S.C.**[489]

"The aim of justice is to discover truth and apply same so as to give meaning to the life of the society."
> **Ignatius Chukwudi Pats-Acholonu, J.S.C.**[490]

"What an appellate court should be interested in, is whether from the entire judgment justice has been done to the parties and in considering this package of justice, an appellate court should not be myopically interested in pockets of irregularities in the judgment but the totality of it all."
> **Christopher Mitchell Chukwuma-Eneh, J.C.A.**[491]

---

[487] Abdullahi v. Elayo (1993) 1 NWLR (Pt. 268) 171 at 195, F
[488] Broad Bank of Nig. Ltd v. Olayiwola (2005) 3 NWLR (Pt. 912) 434 at 457, H
[489] Green v. Green (1987) NSCC (Vol. 18) 1115 at 1143, 48-51
[490] Buhari v. Obasanjo (2005) 13 NWLR (Pt. 941) 1 at 281, B
[491] Ushae v. COP (2005) 11 NWLR (Pt. 937) 499 at 533-534H-A quoting Lord Denning, MR in his book "The Family Story"

"Justice in our system is one in accordance with the law. Sentiments have no place where justice is so administered."
Musa Dattijo Muhammad, J.C.A.[492]

"There is no justice in exercising jurisdiction where there is none. It is injustice to the law, to the court and to the parties so to do."
Andrews Otutu Obaseki, J.S.C.[493]

"All human beings - male and female - are born into a free world and are expected to participate freely, without any inhibition on the grounds of sex; and that is constitutional. Any form of societal discrimination on grounds of sex, apart from being unconstitutional, is antithesis to a society built on the tenets of democracy which we have freely chosen as a people."
Niki Tobi, J.C.A.[494]

"To terminate a case when no pleading has been filed is to try and short circuit administration of justice by a method of wait and take characterization of adjudication which turns the administration of justice into a charade."
Ignatius Chukwudi Pats-Acholonu, J.C.A.[495]

"To leave the attainment of justice to a free-for-all pursuit and jettison the rule is to pave way for judicial high-handedness and the omnipotence of individual judges."
Pius Olayiwola Aderemi, J.C.A.[496]

---

[492] Nwosu v. Minister of Housing (2005) 11 NWLR (Pt. 937) 441 at 459, G
[493] Oloba v. Akereja (1988) 7 SC (Pt.1) 1 at 11-12
[494] Mojekwu v. Mojekwu (1997) 7 NWLR (Pt.512) 283 at 305, A-B
[495] Republic Bank Ltd v. CBN (1998) 13 NWLR (Pt.581) 306 at 332, E
[496] Adeboanu Manufacturing Ind. (Nig.) Ltd v. Akiyode (2000) 13 NWLR (Pt. 685) 576 at 588, C

"The standard of capricious and unreasonable people should not be allowed to determine and control the legal aphorism that justice must not only be seen to be done; but must be manifestly seen to be done; otherwise judicial or quasi-judicial functions would be almost impossible to perform."

Samson Odemwingie Uwaifo, J.S.C.[497]

"...the principles enshrined in the law of contempt are there to uphold and ensure the effective administration of justice."

Pius Olayiwola Aderemi, J.C.A.[498]

"Justice is a valuable commodity. Rules, and principles of courts, practice and the substantive law define the mode and set the limits of what efforts we are free to make in order to get that 'justice' in the event of need. The existence of these rules, these laws, these principles make the quest for and the route to justice fully clear and certain."

Musa Dattijo Muhammad, J.C.A.[499]

"It remains to say that it is unquestionably in tune with modern trend towards the notion of technicality that there has arisen a shift from the earlier rigid attitude of the courts. Today, therefore, this shift deprecates undue adherence to technicalities in legal proceedings which tend to stultify progress in legal development and such quibbling that tend to put the law in poor light in the estimation of the unsuspecting citizenry, and which should be much deprecated.... the era of undue adherence to technicality has now waned."

Okay Achike, J.C.A.[500]

---

[497] The Secretary, Iwo Central L.G. v. Adio (2000) 8 NWLR (Pt.667) 115 at 153, B
[498] Fame Publication Ltd v. Encomium Ventures Ltd (2000) 8 NWLR (Pt. 667) 105 at 111, D-E
[499] Menkita v. Menkita (2000) 8 NWLR (Pt.667) 154 at 169, A-B
[500] Anatogu v. Anatogu (1997) 9 NWLR (Pt.519) 49 at 69, G-H

10 SUPREMACY OF THE CONSTITUTION

"...The fair hearing provision in the Constitution is the machinery or locomotive of justice; not a spare part to propel or invigorate the case of the user. It is not a casual principle of law available to a party to be picked up at will in a case and force the court to apply it to his advantage. On the contrary, it is a formidable and fundamental constitutional *provision available to a party who is really denied fair hearing because he was not heard or that he was not properly heard in the case.*"

Chima Centus Nweze J.S.C.[501]

"The Constitution is the barometer on which the constitutionality or otherwise of a statute is measured. Where a statute is inconsistent or in conflict with any provision of the constitution, the provision of the statute will be null and void. This essentially the language of Section 1 (3) of the Constitution (*Constitution of the Federal Republic of Nigeria, 1999*).

Before a court of law can declare a whole statute as inconsistent with the Constitution and therefore a nullity, the court must examine the totality of the statute very carefully. This is important because a court of law has no jurisdiction to declare a whole statute a nullity if some provisions are not inconsistent with the Constitution."

Niki Tobi, J. S. C.[502]

"In trying to interpret the words of the Constitution, I am of the humble view that it should be understood that a Constitution is not a mere common legal document. It is essentially a document relating to and regulating the affairs of the nation state and stating the functions and powers of the different apparati of the Government as well as regulating the relationship between the

---

[501] Kolo v. C.O.P. (2017) 9 NWLR (Pt.1569) 118 at 157-158, D-C
[502] A. G. Lagos State v. A. G. Federation (2003) 12 NWLR (Pt.833) 1 at 244 paras. A-C

citizen and the State. It equally makes provisions for the rights of the citizen within the compass of the State."

Ignatius Chukwudi Pats-Acholonu, J.C. A.[503]

"Under the 1999 Constitution of Nigeria, fair hearing is guaranteed to a litigant but it does not operate to force a litigant to utilize such opportunity or force the opposing party or even the Court to grind to a halt if the party to whom the opportunity has been offered chooses not to utilize same. In other words, the rule of fair hearing does not extend to where a person has misused the opportunity given to him to ventilate his grievances at the hearing of his case."

Jimi Olukayode Bada, J. C. A.[504]

"Due process must be followed to establish the guilt of an accused. The prosecution must not ride rough-shod of the Constitution and it is sacred duty to the Judge not to bow to public sentiment in finding an accused person guilty. After all we operate the accusatorial system of jurisprudence where an accused is presumed innocent until he is proved guilty."

Kumai Bayang Aka'ahs, J.S.C.[505]

"My understanding of the type of the Constitution we are operating is that the Constitution is the mirror upon which our action or the actions of the National Assembly or any other public institution must be assessed. All actions must reflect the Constitution or else they will be considered as nullity. That being the case, we have to look and see if the said Constitution has made provisions on a particular subject matter then, no other body can enlarge, alter and curtail the provisions of the Constitution.

---

[503] Abaribe v. Abia State House of Assembly (2002) 14 NWLR (Pt.788) 466 at 486 paras. D-F
[504] Prince Abubakar & 22 Ors v. INEC &Ors. EPR Vol. 9 414 at 533 See Electronic Law
[505] Maideribe v. FRN (2014) 5 NWLR (Pt. 1399) 68 at 99-100 paras H-A

Since we all agree that the Constitution of the Federal Republic of Nigeria, 1999 is the basic law of our country Nigeria, it is therefore a simple logic that its provisions must have binding force on all authorities, institutions and persons throughout Nigeria consistently with the above any action, legislation by the National Assembly and guidelines by the INEC which are inconsistent with same would definitely be struck out or shall I say "struck down" for inconsistency."

Muntaka-Coomassie, Mohammed Saifullahi, J.C.A.[506]

"It is essential to state that in Nigeria, we operate only one constitution and regards of the 1st Respondent that in some instances, the Federal High Court can treat a State High Court as a foreign Court, the Federal High Court by the nature of the powers conferred on it by the Constitution still operate in the same hierarchy duly recognized by the Constitution. The parties cannot conveniently obey the respective orders made by the two Courts at the same as that will amount to doing the impossibility."

Ignatius Chukwudi Pats-Acholonu, J. S.C.[507]

"Where the National Assembly has the power under the Constitution to legislate on a matter, it can only do so within the provisions and in full compliance with the provisions of the Constitution. Any legislation which is inconsistent with those provisions is null and void and inoperative."

Kalgo, Umaru Atu, J.S.C.[508]

"Where a party considered that his constitutional rights have been breached, that party can quite properly seek the invocation

---
[506] Musa v. INEC (2002) 11 NWLR (Pt.778) 223 at 309-310 paras. F-B
[507] N I M B Ltd. v. U B N (2004) 12 NWLR (Pt.888) 599 at 619 paras. E-F
[508] A. G. Abia State v. A. G. Fed. (2002) 6 NWLR (Pt.763) 264 at 487 paras. A-B

of the Court's powers to protect the invasion of such rights. If the Constitution is to be upheld, and undoubtedly it must be then a breached or the likelihood of its being breached must be capable of not only being vindicated but also of being prevented."

Akintola, Olufemi Ejiwunmi, J.S.C.[509]

"The Court must do all it can to jealously guard its power and the Supremacy of our constitution as the grundnorm, which is, and above all other authorities. The Court, as the custodian of the Constitution must not therefore be seen to ridicule the very institution that puts it in place."

Clara Bata Ogunbiyi, J.S.C.[510]

"The Constitution is supreme and what it has stipulated remains sacrosanct, immutable and nothing to do about it but to strictly comply."

Mary Ukaego Peter-Odili, J.S.C.[511]

"Political parties must do all that is possible to ensure adherence to the provisions of their Constitution so as to encourage Nigerians to be confident in entrusting the protection and enforcement of the provisions of the Nigerian Constitution into their hands. Where a political party refuses or neglects to abide by the provisions of its Constitution in its relationship with its members we have the beginning of the culture of impunity and with it, chaos, uncertainty and indiscipline; which should not be encouraged."

Walter Samuel Nkanu Onnoghen, C.J.N.[512]

---

[509] A. G. Adamawa State v. A. G. Fed. (2005) 18 NWLR (Pt.958) 581 at 654 paras B-C
[510] Okorocha v. PDP (2014) 7 NWLR (Pt.1406) 213 at 269 paras C-D
[511] Ugba v. Suswam (2014) 14 NWLR (Pt.1427) 264 at 345 paras. C-D
[512] Lau v. P.D.P (2018) 4 NWLR (Pt.1608) 123 at paras. E-F

"It has been reiterated by this court time and time again that retraction of a confessional statement does not automatically vitiate its admission as a voluntary statement. There can be no account of the commission of a crime more accurate than the account of an accused person narrating how the offence was committed and the role he played."

Kudirat Motonmori Olatokunbo Kekere-Ekun, J.S.C.[513]

"By the underlined portion of section 251(1) of the Constitution the executive jurisdiction conferred by that section on the Federal High Court is not exhaustive. An act of the National Assembly may confer further or additional exclusive jurisdiction on that court."

Nwali Sylvester Ngwuta, J.S.C.[514]

"Indeed, what has occurred and which the court of Appeal decried in its judgment is that there has been a classic case of abuse of court process with the appellant in forum shopping adventure to steal a march on the 1st respondent in an irritating and vexation manner."

Mary Ukaego Peter-Odili, J.S.C.[515]

"It would amount to an abuse of process when a party improperly uses the judicial process to interfere negatively with the due administration of justice such a proceeding would be frivolous and pollutes the streams of justice which must remain pure always."

Bode Rhodes-Vivour, J.S.C.[516]

---

[513] Ogedengbe v. State (2014) 12 NWLR (Pt.1421) at 384 paras. B-C
[514] Lokpobiri v. Ogola (2016) 3 NWLR (Pt.1499) at 372 para C
[515] Lokpobiri v. Ogola (2016) 3 NWLR (Pt.1499) at 384 paras. D-G
[516] Lokpobiri v. Ogola (2016) 3 NWLR (Pt.1499) at 370 paras. F-G

"No matter how tardy a party might be in the prosecution or defence of his case before the court, he has constittional right guaranteed by section 36(1) of the 1999 Constitution to be notified of the dates when the cause or matter will be heard."

Kudirat Motonmori Olatokunbo Kekere-Ekun J.S.C.[517]

"The Constitution of any country is usually called the organic law or grundnorm of the people. It is the formulation of all the laws from which the institutions of State derive their creation and legitimacy. It is the unifying force in the nation and it apportions rights and imposes obligations on the people who are subject to its operations."

Walter Samuel Nkanu Onnoghen, J.S.C.[518]

---

[517] Achuzia v. Ogbomah (2016) 11 NWLR (Pt.1522) 59 at 81 para. H
[518] A-G Federation v. Abubakar (2007) 10 NWLR (Pt.1041) 1 at 118, G-H

11 THE EXECUTIVE AND THE RULE OF LAW

"Instructively, implicit in the judicial oath subscribed to by all of us judicial officers, fundamentally requires a total commitment to the rule of law, to the dispensation of justice according to law, without fear and favour, affection or ill-will, honestly, faithfully, and according to the Constitution and the laws made pursuant thereto".
Ibrahim Mohammed Musa Saulawa, J.C.A.[519]

"Public service is a sacred trust and an Attorney-General should epitomize all that is good and noble in the legal profession. That office should never again be occupied by individuals of such poor quality as the appellant".
Joseph Olubunmi Kayode Oyewole, J.C.A.[520]

"I have to say that Administrators who are to deal with citizens should be even-handed and impartial. One commissioner gave the Respondent land and his successor peremptorily took it from him. There must be appearance of the rule of law not the rule of whims and caprice in the management of human affairs. This is how civilized government should function."
Helen Moronkeji Ogunwumiju, J.C.A.[521]

"The immunity enjoyed by the executive heads of government at the state and federal levels by virtue of our constitution is not intended to foster corruption or make the beneficiaries of such immunity impudent and above the law. It is certainly not the purport of that provision, for the beneficiaries of the said immunity to hide behind the constitution and offend the law."
Denton-West, Sotonye, J.C.A.[522]

---

[519] Makarfi v. Poroye (2017) 10 NWLR (Pt.1574) 419 at 440-441; 425, G-D
[520] Aondoaka v. Obot (2016) 6 NWLR (Pt.1508) 280 at 327; 328, F-B
[521] Eleran v. Aderonpe (2008) 11 NWLR (Pt.1097) 50 at 79 paras. F-G
[522] Alamieyeseigha v. F. R. N. (2006) 16 NWLR (Pt.1004) 1 at 127 paras. A-E

"It is in the public interest that the expenditure of public funds be done in a manner that accords with due process as prescribed by law, to ensure accountability and transparency. Government expenditure for the public good must be in an organized or regulated manner in accordance with the Appropriation Law of the State. This is the only way to guarantee efficient and effective implementation of State budgets for the maximum public good to ensure good governance."

Abdul-Kadir, Abubakar Jega, J.C.A.[523]

"Any person who is at the corridors of Local Government finances or funds or in some proximity with such finances or funds or sleeping with them and sees this judgment as a victory in the sense that he has the freedom of the air to steal from the finances or funds, should think twice and quickly remind himself that the two anti-corruption bodies, the Independent Corrupt Practices Commission (ICPC) and the Economic and Financial Crimes Commission (EFCC), are watching him very closely and will, without notice, pounce on him for incarceration after due process. But that is not as serious as God's Law which says he will go to hell and he will certainly make hell. This is not a curse. God's law does not lie because God is not a liar."

Niki Tobi, J.S.C.[524]

"Our executive must wake up and realize that the law is not a political instrument that should be circumvented to score political goals in the game of politics. The executive must know that he who comes to equity must come with clean hands. The government must not only respect the law, it must in fact submit to the law in total. The government may not rightly choose

---

[523] Azubuike v. Government of Enugu State (2014) 5 NWLR (Pt.1400) 364 at 397 paras B-D
[524] A.G. Abia State & 2 Ors. v. A. G. Federation & 33 Ors. (2006) 16 NWLR (Pt.1005) 265 at 389, G-H

which law to abide by and which law to flaunt or when to abide by the law and when not to be law abiding. The executive ought at all times to respect the law and follow legal procedures. It is the challenge of the government to govern by example."

Denton-West, Sotonye, J. C. A.[525]

"If the Federal Government felt aggrieved by Lagos State creating more Local Governments, the best solution is to seek redress in a court of law, without resorting to self-help. In a society where the rule of law prevails, self-help is not available to the Executive or any arm of government. In view of the fact that such a conduct could breed anarchy and totalitarianism and since anarchy and totalitarianism are antithesis to democracy, courts operating the rule of law, the life blood of democracy, are under a constitutional duty to stand against such action."

Niki Tobi, J.S.C.[526]

---

[525] Alamieyeseigha v. F. R. N. (2006) 16 NWLR (Pt.1004) 1 at 127-128 paras G-A
[526] A.G., Lagos State v. A. G., Federation (2004) 18 NWLR (Pt.904) 1 at 127 paras. D-G

12 THE SUPREME COURT AND THE ADVANCEMENT OF THE LAW

"In our organic law, where the Supreme Court in particular, watches with hawk-like guard on the kind of laws passed by our legislature, it will be remiss on its part to ignore an enactment that actually seeks to invade the preserve of the judiciary."

Ignatius Chukwudi Pats-Acholonu, J.S.C.[527]

"The Supreme Court possesses inherent power to set aside its judgment in appropriate cases but that such inherent jurisdiction cannot be converted into an appellate jurisdiction as though the matter before it is another appeal, intended to afford the losing litigants yet another opportunity to re-state or re-argue their appeal."

John Iyang Okoro, J.S.C.[528]

"....It is not for the Supreme Court or any other court in the land to add to or subtract from what the Constitution has provided. The courts are enjoined to give effect to the clear plain and unambiguous stipulations in the Constitution."

Mary Peter-Odili, J.S.C.[529]

"A party should thus be consistent in stating his case and consistent in proving it.... Justice is much more than a game of hide and seek. It is an attempt, our human imperfection notwithstanding to discover the truth.... A party is to be consistent with the case he sets up and not shift ground in another court as it suits his fancy."

Bode Rhodes-Vivour, J.S.C.[530]

---

[527] A. G. Adamawa State v. A. G. Fed. (2005) 18 NWLR [Pt.958] 581 at 667 para E-F
[528] Citee Int'l Estates Ltd v. Francis (2014) 8 NWLR (Pt.1408) 139 at 159, C-D
[529] Nyako v. A.S.H.A. (2017) 6 NWLR (Pt.1562) 347 at 412, paras. F-G
[530] Nyako v. A.S.H.A. (2017) 6 NWLR (Pt.1562) 347, at 403 paras. E-F; H See also: Ajide v. Kelani (1985) 3 NWLR (Pt.12) page 248

"Provisions of the Constitution are to be applied and not rewritten by the court and so no court has the power to extend the period of four years prescribed for the Governor of a state beyond his terminal date in office."

Bode Rhodes-Vivour, J.S.C.[531]

"Law making in the strict sense of that term is not the function of the judiciary but that of the legislature. To accede to a prayer of the Plaintiff/Appellant and read the word 'uninterrupted' into the provision of the Constitution now under consideration will be for the judicial arm of government to engage in an unwelcome trespass into the territory of the legislative arm of government."

Pius Olayiwola Aderemi, J.S.C.[532]

"Occasionally the law passed by the legislators may not meet the modern day requirements. It may be defective. Let that defect be put right by the legislators. A judge is far better employed if he puts himself to the much singular task of deciding what the law is."

Pius Olayiwola Aderemi, J.S.C.[533]

---

[531] Nyako v. A.S.H.A. (2017) 6 NWLR (Pt.1562) at 404-405, paras. H-A
[532] Ladoja v. INEC (2007) 12 NWLR (Pt.1047) 115 at 189, paras. C-D
[533] Ladoja v. INEC (2007) 12 NWLR (Pt.1047) at 115. Referred to by Mohammad, J.S.C - Nyako v. A.S.H.A. (2017) 6 NWLR (Pt.1562) 347 at 400, A-B

13 MISCELLANY

"It has become a fashion for litigants to resort to their right to fair hearing on appeal as if it is a magic wand to cure all their inadequacies at the trial court. But it is not so and cannot be so....".

Niki Tobi J.S.C.[534]

"The principles enshrined in the law of contempt are there to uphold and ensure the effective administration of justice. They are the means by which the law vindicates public interest in due administration of justice."

Abimbola Osarugue Obaseki-Adejumo, J.C.A.[535]

"Lack of internal democracy in the political parties is a serious threat to democracy in the country".

Nwali Sylvester Ngwuta J.S.C.[536]

"When two vehicles are going in the same direction on the highway one after the other and the one at the rear hits the one in front of it, the presumption is that the driver of the rear vehicle drove negligently."

Salihu Modibbo Alfa Belgore, J.S.C.[537]

"The proprietary of employing a used aircraft that had remained stationary and unused for commercial air transportation is to say the least mind boggling and quite frightening. I would imagine that even a brand new aircraft or indeed any other machinery that had remained inoperative for such a long time would have serious maintenance and repair problems and this may well be part of the explanation for the rather frequent air mishaps in this

---

[534] Orugbo v Una (2002) 16 NWLR (Pt.792) 175 at 211-212, H-C
[535] J.B. Estate Development & Properties Ltd v. Nzegwu (N0.2) (2016) 6 NWLR (Pt.1507) 117 at 158, G-H
[536] Ogbuego v. P.D.P 2016 4 NWLR (Pt.1503) 446 at 486 F-G
[537] Eseigbe v. Agholor (1993) 9 NWLR (Pt.316) 128 at 141-142, H-A

country. It has become imperative for the authorities to take a closer look at this area of public transportation..."
Stanley Shenko Alagoa, J.C.A.[538]

"Litigations are contest between opposing claimants over stated rights. But rights do not loom at large. They are necessarily tied to the subject matter of the litigation between the parties who are in disagreement over the realities and genuineness of their opposing claims."
Musa Dattijo Muhammad, J.C.A.[539]

"A society which breeds student armed robbers is in a big danger in terms of instability and disequilibrium. The child's life begins and starts from the home. One way of avoiding the malady is for the parents to inculcate serious moral lessons."
Niki Tobi, J.S.C.[540]

"No doubt, government, especially of a nation and taxation are essential bed fellows. Indeed, it is said that Government has two sources of funding viz: taxation and loan. It follows therefore that Government has the inherent power to legislate on and impose tax. However, this inherent power cannot be left at large in a huge federating union like our great nation Nigeria."
Monica Bolna'an Dongban-Mensem, J.C.A.[541]

"Taxation should be a tool of social engineering, of societal class structure adjustment in the hands of a responsive and sensitive government."
Monica Bolna'an Dongban-Mensem, J.C.A.[542]

---

[538] FIPDC (Nig.) Ltd v. EAS Ltd (2006) 6 NWLR (Pt.975) 1 at 25, H-A
[539] Nwosu v. Minister of Housing (2005) 11 NWLR (Pt.937) 441 at 457, H
[540] Dibie v. State (2007) 9 NWLR (Pt.1038) 30 at 57, G
[541] Eti-Osa Local Govt v. Jegede (2007) 10 NWLR (Pt.1043) 537 at 558, F-G
[542] Eti-Osa Local Govt v. Jegede (2007) 10 NWLR (Pt.1043) 537 at 559, B

"Today, the main thrust of case law is not only to ensure substantial justice, but also to save valuable time and money for litigant in the pursuit of justice."

Amina Adamu Augie, J.C.A.[543]

"The dailies are littered with gory details of extra judicial killings by trigger happy policemen on our roads especially at checkpoints. A trigger happy police force is not good police force. There is the dire need for the training and retraining of the Nigerian Police Force if is to take its place among the civilized Police Forces in the world."

Stanley Shenko Alagoa, J.S.C.[544]

"The court is not Father Christmas to dole out gifts not asked for by children. Even Father Christmas is generous with his gifts only on Christmas day."

Niki Tobi, J.S.C.[545]

"I do not think that it can be repeated too often that every employer, including every public body must be careful not to abdicate or to abuse its powers. Employers and public bodies are required by law, at all times, to act in good faith and reasonably and fairly towards people and matters under their charge in all circumstances… In the determination of the employment of employees, they must at all times allow themselves to be guided by the rule of natural justice."

Nzeako, Ifeyinwa Cecilia, J.C.A.[546]

---

[543] Akintaro v. Eegungbohun (2007) 9 NWLR (Pt.1038) 103 at 123 paras. B-C
[544] Ononuju v. State (2014) 8 NWLR (Pt.1409) 345 at 395 paras D-E
[545] A.G. Abia State & 2 Ors. v. A. G. Federation & 33 Ors. (2006) 16 NWLR (Pt.1005) 265 at 388 paras. H
[546] UMTHMB v. Dawa (2001) 16 NWLR (Pt.739) 424 at 448 paras. E-G

"It is essential that honour and decency form an integral part of commercial transactions to foster needed economic developments."

Joseph Olubunmi Kayode Oyewole, J.C.A.[547]

"The test of a reasonable person in Nigeria courts is not that of a person whose mind and thoughts are coloured by political, sectional or other primordial considerations. Such a reasonable person is one who is able to weigh his observations objectively. Fundamentally, such reasonable person is one who is present in court at the trial and must therefore arrive at a conclusion from his observations in court and not based on other events outside the court."

Tsammani, Haruna Simon, J.C.A.[548]

"The philosophy behind frontloading procedure is to quicken the dispensation of justice and that Judges of the High Court where such procedure is adopted are no longer adjudicators and/or umpire or interested in the trial of disputes in the courtroom only but have become managerial Judges who must effectually utilize the technique and tool of case management and judicial control to achieve/facilitate just, efficient and speedy dispensation of justice."

Ignatius Igwe Agube, J.C.A.[549]

"The Constitution of the Federal Republic of Nigeria is the supreme law, the fountains of all laws. It provides for fundamental rights but members of the Armed Forces and the Police, who are very much Nigerians too, have in some cases their rights curtailed. They have no say when, ordered to war fronts or to

---

[547] Dugeri v. Vee-Networks Ltd (2015) 2 NWLR (Pt.1442) 30 at 49 paras. D-E
[548] Daniel v. F.R.N (2014) 8 NWLR (Pt.1410) 570 at 617 paras. A - D
[549] Olaniyan v. Oyewole (2008) 5 NWLR (Pt.1079) 114 at 146 paras. A-B

face riotous and dangerous crowds. With the possibility of death and serious injuries they are bound to obey superior orders in lawful deployment. This is so because national security and territorial and sovereign integrity of Nigeria is of paramount and strategic importance than individual freedom."

Salihu Modibbo Alfa Belgore, J.S.C.[550]

"We must not lose sight of the fact that the universities exist to train future responsible leaders of our great nation and that one of the conditions which they must fulfill before being presented as graduates is that they must be found worthy in learning and character. Therefore if the character of a student is doubtful due to its arrest and prosecution by the relevant agencies it is only reasonable for the university authorities to play safe by taking the necessary steps under the enabling enactment to save guard its reputation by not graduating a student who is later convicted and sentenced by a Court of competent jurisdiction or graduating an ex-convict."

Walter Samuel Nkanu Onnoghen, J. C. A.[551]

"In introducing the front loading system, (the upfront filing of all documents to be used at the trial is so called) the intention of the maker of the rules of court is to ensure that only serious and committed litigants with *prima facie* good cases and witnesses to back up their claim would come to court and fewer lame duck claims would find their way into court.

However, there must be a happy medium between balancing the public interest to reduce unnecessary and frivolous claims

---

[550] Okike v. L.P.D.C. (2005) 15 NWLR (Pt. 949) 471 at 520 paras. F-H
[551] University of Ilorin v. UBN PLC (2002) 3 NWLR (Pt.755) 626 at 646 paras. A-C

as against the constitutional right of a party to have his legal counsel conduct his case as he thinks fit."

Helen Moronkeji Ogunwumiju, J.C.A.[552]

"It is the duty of counsel representing an accused person, especially one facing a capital offence to use all resources at his disposal; by this I mean his knowledge of the law to ensure that the accused person has the best defence possible. For counsel not to put forward the defence of insanity on these facts is unbelievable. It is clear that the defence was handled in a shoddy manner devoid of seriousness, and this attitude is condemned in the strongest terms."

Bode Rhodes-Vivour, J.S.C.[553]

"The action of the Federal Government that brought about pre-shipment inspection of goods that were imported into the country was to bring sanity to the economy of this country (Nigeria). Therefore, agents who are appointed to carry out this assignment owe this nation and all those involved in the exportation and importation of goods to and from this country a duty of care in the performance of their duty."

Galinje, Paul Adamu, J.C.A.[554]

"It is about time something is done to curtail the excesses of trigger happy policemen. The police authorities must go extra mile to ensure that constant checks are carried out on policemen who carry guns, and these checks should include constant examination by a psychiatrist."

Bode Rhodes-Vivour, J.C.A.[555]

---

[552] Olaniyan v. Oyewole (2008) 5 NWLR (Pt.1079) 114 at 138 paras. E-F
[553] Adelu v. State (2014) 13 NWLR (Pt.1425) 465 at 490 paras. E-G
[554] ISC Services Ltd. v. G.C. Ltd. (2006) 6 NWLR (Pt. 977) 481 at 510 paras. A-D
[555] Oyakhare v. State (2005) 15 N.W.L.R. (Pt.947) 180 Paras. F-H

"When a Judge finds that there is a case to answer, it makes sense to keep the ruling brief. It is permissible for the ruling to simply read: "There is a case to answer"
Bode Rhodes-Vivour, J.S.C.[556]

"There is no hard and fast rule or set standard in the style or writing of a judgment. Every judge has the freedom to use the style or method suitable for his purpose, I dare say a peculiar style which enables him perform that duty of judgment writing without undue fuss or stress."
Mary Ukaego Peter-Odili, J.S.C.[557]

"No one but a Daniel will go to a lion's den without expecting to be devoured. In the same vein, making a slanderous speech at a press conference held at a press centre is like feeding gratuitously an unwary reporter with juicy news for publication."
Ephraim Omorose Ibukun Akpata, J.S.C.[558]

"…I need to state it that interim injunction order is not meant to provide a temporary victory to be used against an adverse party ad infinitum. It should not be allowed to hang on the opposing side like the proverbial sword of Damocles… It must not be granted to humiliate the other party."
John Afolabi Fabiyi, J.C.A.[559]

"…an attempt to hoodwink the Court with highfalutin phrases used by expert writers to bamboozle the court should not make

---

[556] Uzoagba v. C.O.P. (2014) 5 NWLR (Pt.1401) 441 at 465 paras. D-F
[557] Mbanefo v. Molokwu (2014) 6 NWLR (Pt.1403) 377 at 416-417 paras. H- B
[558] Mueller v. Mueller (2006) 6 NWLR (Pt.977) 627 at 645 paras. F-G
[559] Alofoje v. F.H.A (1996) 6 NWLR (Pt.456) 559 at 568, C-D

the court fall for such false abracadabra and lend itself to unwholesome belief."

Ignatius Chukwudi Pats-Acholonu, J.C.A.[560]

"Husband and wife, given the changes sweeping across our society today, in so far as the rights and duties to make financial provisions are concerned, albeit in theory, are gradually moving towards equal footing base. Many wives are today more financially empowered than their husbands. And so the courts are fast moving away from the old rule whereby they virtually ordered financial provisions in favour of the wife. Law, to be useful, must always reflect the norms and development stages reached in a society where it will apply."

Pius Olayiwola Aderemi, J.C.A.[561]

"The interest of justice demands that as far as possible the common issues between the parties should be determined once and for all so as to avoid multiplicity of proceedings."

Dahiru Musdapher, J.C.A.[562]

"…it cannot be seriously suggested that there is anything secret in the teachings of Jesus Christ which in my view are entirely public and properly documented in scriptures, clearly to assert… that Jesus Christ was a member of secret societies and that he was an advocate of occult teaching is, speaking for myself, satanic, sinister, blasphemous and entirely unacceptable."

Anthony Ikechukwu Iguh, J.S.C.[563]

---

[560] Registered Trustee of Amorc v. Awoniyi (1994) 7 NWLR (Pt.355) 154 at 19, G
[561] Nwaigwe v. Okere (2008) 13 NWLR (Pt.1105) 445 at 479, C-D
[562] NTA v. Babatope (1996) 4 NWLR (Pt.440) 75 at 90, G-H
[563] Obeta v. Okpe (1996) 9 NWLR (Pt.473) 401 at 456, G

"Appeals are not won on the quantity of issues but on their quality. While a well thought out and well framed single issue can win an appeal, bogus, verbose and rigmarole issues will not."

Niki Tobi, J.S.C.[564]

"The law in its wisdom insists that words which are capable of leaving a stain on the reputation of another should not in the absence of lawful excuse be uttered or published of or concerning a person."

Ignatius Chukwudi Pats-Acholonu, J.C.A.[565]

"I must say the obvious that the Head of State is an extremely busy man grappling with numerous and enormous State duties and in our present peculiar Nigerian situation, it is a most difficult schedule. I think initiators of Decrees should sympathise with the daily schedule of the Head of State and reduce to the minimum the amendments they seek in respect of Decrees."

Niki Tobi, J.C.A.[566]

---

[564] Ejabulor v. Osha (1990) 5 NWLR (Pt.148) 1 at 14, E-F
[565] Okeke v. Okoli (2000) 1 NWLR (Pt.642) 641 at 655, D
[566] Chukwu Const. Co. Ltd v. Uwechia (2000) 2 NWLR (Pt. 643) 92 at 99, F

LIST OF CASES IN ALPHABETICAL ORDER

1. A.G Ondo State v. AG Federation (2002) 9 NWLR (Pt.772) 222 at 364, G-H
2. A.G Ondo State v. AG Federation and 19 Ors (1983) 2 SCNLR 269 at 277
3. A.G. Abia State & 2 Ors. v. A. G. Federation & 33 Ors. (2006) 16 NWLR (Pt.1005) 265 at 389, G-H
4. A.G. Abia State & 2 Ors. v. A. G. Federation & 33 Ors. (2006) 16 NWLR (Pt.1005) 265 at 388 paras. H
5. A.G. Abia State v. A. G. Fed. (2002) 6 NWLR (Pt.763) 264 at 487 paras. A-B
6. A.G. Adamawa State v. A.G. Fed. (2005) 18 NWLR (Pt.958) 581 at 667 para E-F
7. A.G. Enugu State v. Omaba (1998) 1 NWLR (Pt. 532) 83 at 101, D
8. A.G. Lagos State v. A. G. Federation (2003) 12 NWLR (Pt.833) 1 at 244 paras. A-C
9. A.G., Federation v. ANPP (2003) 18 (Pt.851) 182 at 215, E
10. A.-G., Federation v. Guardian Newspaper Ltd (1999) 9 NWLR (Pt.618) 187 at 239, E
11. A.-G., Federation v. Guardian Newspaper Ltd (1999) 9 NWLR (Pt.618) 187 at 255, F
12. A.G., Lagos State v. A. G., Federation (2004) 18 NWLR (Pt.904) 1 at 127 paras. D-G

List of Cases in Alphabetical Order

13. Abacha v. FRN (2006) 4 NWLR (Pt.970) 239 at 311, B-C
14. Abaribe v. Abia State House of Assembly (2002) 14 NWLR (Pt.788) 466 at 486 paras. D-F
15. Abaye v. Ofili (1986) 1 NWLR (Pt.15) 134 at 160, G
16. Abdullahi v. Elayo (1993) 1 NWLR (Pt. 268) 171 at 195, F
17. ACB Ltd v. Nnamani (1991) 4 NWLR (Pt.186) 486 at 495, E-F
18. ACB Ltd v. Nnamani (1991) 4 NWLR (Pt.186) 486 at 496, E
19. ACB Ltd. v. Nnamani (1991) 4 NWLR (Pt.186) 486 at 494, G
20. Access Bank Plc v. MFCCS (2005) 3 NWLR (Pt.913) 460 at 474
21. Achebe v. Nwosu (2003) 7 NWLR (Pt.818) 103 at 135, H
22. Achuzia v. Ogbomah (2016) 11 NWLR (Pt.1522) 59 at 81 para. H
23. Adamu v. A.G. Borno State (1996) 8 NWLR (Pt.465) 203 at 223, H
24. Adamu v. A.G. Borno State (1996) 8 NWLR (Pt.465) 203 at 223, H quoting Kania, CJ in Gopalan v. State of Madras (1950) SCR 88 at 109
25. Adava v. State (2006) 9 NWLR (Pt.984) 152 at 177, F-G
26. Adava v. State (2006) 9 NWLR (Pt.984) 152 at 178, H (Dissenting Opinion)
27. Adebayo v. Shogo (2005) 7 NWLR (Pt.925) 467 at 481, H
28. Adeboanu Manufacturing Ind. (Nig.) Ltd v. Akiyode (2000) 13 NWLR (Pt. 685) 576 at 588, C
29. Adelu v. State (2014) 13 NWLR (Pt.1425) 465 at 490 paras. E-G
30. Adeniji v. State (1992) 4 NWLR (Pt.234) 248 at 265, H-A
31. Adeniyi v. Oroja (1992) 4 NWLR (Pt.235) 322 at 343, E
32. Adeogun v. Fashogbon (2008) 17 NWLR (Pt. 1115) 149 at 175E-G re-emphasising the decision of Aniagolu, J.S.C.

in Adeyemi (Alafin of Oyo) v. A.-G., Oyo State (1984) 1 SCNLR 525 at 602, G
33. Adeogun v. Fashogbon (2008) 17 NWLR (Pt.1115) 149 at 174, G-H
34. Adeogun v. Fashogbon (2008) 17 NWLR (Pt.1115) 149 at 175, E-G re-emphasising the decision of Aniagolu, J.S.C. in Adeyemi (Alafin of Oyo) v. A.-G., Oyo State (1984) 1 SCNLR 525 at 602, E-F
35. Adeogun v. Fashogbon (2008) 17 NWLR (Pt.1115) 149 at 180, G-H
36. Adeogun v. Fashogbon (2008) 17 NWLR (Pt.1115) 149 at 201, F-G
37. Adewunmi v. A.-G., Ondo State (1996) 8 NWLR (Pt.464) 73 at 91, G
38. Afisi v. Lawal (1992) 1 NWLR (Pt.217) 350 at 366, G
39. Afric Mining Co. Ltd v. N.I.D.B. Ltd (2000) 2 NWLR (Pt.646) 618 at 629, A-B
40. African Petroleum Ltd v. Owodunni (1991) 8 NWLR (Pt.210) 391 at 417, B
41. A-G Federation v. Abubakar (2007) 10 NWLR (Pt.1041) 1 at 118, G-H
42. A-G Federation v. Guardian Newspaper Ltd (1999) 9 NWLR (Pt.618) 187 at 214, F-G
43. A-G. Federation v. Ajayi (1996) 5 NWLR (Pt.448) 283 at 290 paras. B-C
44. A-G., Anambra State v. A-G., Federation (2005) 9 NWLR (Pt.931) 572 at 638, H
45. Agbabiaka v. FBN Plc (2007) 6 NWLR (Pt.1029) 25 at 44, F
46. Agbai v. Okogbue (1991) 7 NWLR (Pt.204) 391 at 417, D
47. Agbaje v. Fashola (2008) 6 NWLR (Pt.1082) 90 at 144, D-F
48. Agbo v. State (2006) 6 NWLR (Pt.977) 545 at C-G
49. Agbonifo v. Aiwereoba (1988) 1 NWLR (Pt.70) 325 at 342, H

List of Cases in Alphabetical Order

50. Agusiobo v. Onyekwelu (2003) 14 NWLR (Pt.839) 34 at 52, H
51. Agwuna III v. Isiadinso (1996) 5 NWLR (Pt.451) 705 at 719, B
52. Agwuna III v. Isiadinso (1996) 5 NWLR (Pt.451) 705 at 719, C
53. Ajidahun v. Ajidahun (2000) 4 NWLR (Pt.654) 605 at 615, E
54. Ajidahun v. State (1991) 9 NWLR (Pt.213) 33 at 54, F
55. Ajide v. Kelani (1985) 3 NWLR (Pt.12) 248 at 269, D
56. Ajikawo v. Ansaldo (Nig.) Ltd (1991) 2 NWLR (Pt.173) 359 at 374, C
57. Ajileye v. Fakayode (1990) 5 NWLR (Pt.148) 92 at 100-101, H-A
58. Akaide v. State (1996) 8 NWLR (Pt.468) 525 at 531, D-E quoting Mohammed Bello, CJN in Engineering Enterprise v. A.-G., Kaduna State (1987) 2 NWLR (Pt. 57) 381 at 391.
59. Akanni v. Olaniyan (2006) 8 NWLR (Pt.983) 531 at 546, B
60. Akibu v. Oduntan (1992) 2 NWLR (Pt.222) 210 at 220-221, H-A
61. Akinbinu v. Oseni (1992) 1 NWLR (Pt.215) 97 at 121-122, H-A
62. Akinfe v. The State (1988) 3 NWLR (Pt.85) 729 at 754, D
63. Akintaro v. Eegungbohun (2007) 9 NWLR (Pt.1038) 103 at 123 paras. B-C
64. Akintunde v. Ojo (2002) 4 NWLR (Pt.757) 284 at page 316, H
65. Akpalakpa v. Igbaibo (1996) 8 NWLR (Pt.468) 533 at 550, C
66. Akpan v. Utin (1996) 7 NWLR (Pt.463) 634 at 672, C
67. Alabi v. Doherty (2005) 18 NWLR (Pt.957) 411 at 437, E-F
68. Alake v. Abalaka (2003) 6 NWLR (Pt.815) 124 at 143

69. Alamieyeseigha v. F.R.N. (2006) 16 NWLR (Pt.1004) 1 at 127-128 paras G-A
70. Alamieyeseigha v. F. R. N. (2006) 16 NWLR (Pt.1004) 1 at 127 paras. A-E
71. Alamieyeseigha v. Igoniwari (No.2) (2007) 7 NWLR (Pt.1034) 524 at 577, C
72. Albion Construction Co. Ltd v. Rao Invest. & Properties Ltd. (1992) 1 NWLR (Pt.219) 583 at 594, C-D
73. Albion Construction Co. Ltd v. Rao Invest. & Properties Ltd (1992) 1 NWLR (Pt.219) 583 at 596, F-G
74. Alofoje v. F.H.A (1996) 6 NWLR (Pt.456) 559 at 568, C-D
75. Alsthom SA v. Saraki (2000) 14 NWLR (Pt.687) 415 at 427 para. B
76. Amadi v. Military Administrator of Imo State (2000) 4 NWLR (Pt.652) 328 at 337, C
77. Amanchukwu v. FRN (2007) 6 NWLR (Pt.1029) 1 at 19, D
78. Amogun v. Adesina (1994) 4 NWLR (Pt.339) 503 at 509, H
79. Anankpela v. Nigerian Army (2000) 13 NWLR (Pt. 684) at 222 paras.D-E
80. Anankpela v. Nigerian Army (2000) 13 NWLR (Pt.684) 224-225, E-F
81. Anason Farms Ltd v. NAL Merchant Bank (1994) 3 NWLR (Pt.331) 241 at 254, A
82. Anatogu v. Anatogu (1997) 9 NWLR (Pt.519) 49 at 69, G-H
83. Ani v. Nna (1996) 4 NWLR (Pt.440) 101 at 120, C
84. Ani v. Nna (1996) 4 NWLR (Pt.440) 101 at 125, H
85. Ani v. Nna (1996) 4 NWLR (Pt.440) 101 at 126, C-D
86. Ani v. Nna (1996) 4 NWLR (Pt.440) 101 at 127-128, H-A
87. Ani v. State (1996) 5 NWLR (Pt.450) 624 at 633, A
88. Anibire v. Womiloju (1993) 5 NWLR (Pt.295) 623 at 636, D
89. Animashaun v. Olojo (1990) 6 NWLR (Pt. 154) 111 at 122, H

List of Cases in Alphabetical Order

90. Ansa v. Cross Lines Ltd (2005) 14 NWLR (Pt. 946) 645 at 668, E-F
91. Anyankpele v. Nigerian Army (2000) 13 NWLR (Pt.684) 209 at 222, D
92. Aondoaka v. Obot (2016) 6 NWLR (Pt.1508) 280 at 327; 328, F-B
93. Apatira v. Lagos Island Local Govt. Council & Ors (2006) 17 (Pt.1007) 46 at 62, E-F
94. Araka v. Egbue (2003) 7 SC 75 at 85
95. Ararume v. INEC (2007) 9 NWLR (Pt.1038) 127 at 157, F
96. Archibong v. Ita (2004) 2 NWLR (Pt.858) 590 at 619H
97. Ari v. Paiko (1997) 10 NWLR (Pt.524) 335 at 356 B-C (quoting Lord Denning in Macfoy v. United Africa Company Limited (1962) AC 152 at 160
98. Ariori v. Muraino (1983) 1 SC 13 at 24
99. Arojoye v. UBA (1986) 2 NWLR (Pt.20) 101 at 111, H
100. Arubo v. Aiyeleru (1993) 3 NWLR (Pt.280) 126 at 142, A
101. Arubo v. Aiyeleru (1993) 3 NWLR (Pt.280) 126 at 143, D
102. Arubo v. Aiyeleru (1993) 3 NWLR (Pt.280) 126 at 147, C
103. Asanya v. State (1991) 3 NWLR (Pt.180) 422 at 475, H-A
104. Aseimo v. Abraham (1994) 8 NWLR (Pt.361) 191 at 222, F
105. Atejioye v. Ayeni (1998) 6 NWLR (Pt.552) 132 at 141C-D
106. Atungwu v. Ochekwu (2000) 1 NWLR (Pt.641) 507 at 518C-D (quoting Lord Denning in McIlkenny v. Chief Constable of West Midlands Police Force (1980) 2 All ER 227 at 235
107. Awodi v. Kagoro (1998) 4 NWLR (Pt.547) 601 at 607 paras. B-C
108. Awuse v. Odili (2003) 18 NWLR (Pt. 851) 116 at 181, E
109. Awuse v. Odili (2003) 18 NWLR (Pt.851) 116 at 179, C
110. Awuse v. Odili (2005) 16 NWLR (Pt.952) 515 at 529, E-H
111. Awuse v. Odili (2005) 16 NWLR (Pt.952) 515 at 541, F-G

112. Ayalogu v. Agu (1998) 1 NWLR (Pt.532) 129 at 144, E
113. Ayalogu v. Agu (2002) 3 NWLR (Pt.753) 168 at 184, B-C
114. Ayorinde v. Kuforiji (2007) 4 NWLR (Pt.1024) 341 at 371, D-E
115. Ayorinde v. Kuforiji (2007) 4 NWLR (Pt.1024) 341 at 373, F-G
116. Azubuike v. Government of Enugu State (2014) 5 NWLR (Pt.1400) 364 at 397 paras B-D
117. Babatunde v. Olatunji (2000) 2 NWLR (Pt.646) 557 at 572, E
118. Bagudu v. FRN (2004) 1 NWLR (Pt. 853) 182 at 206, E-F
119. Bakare v. Lagos State Civil Service Commission (1992) 8 NWLR (Pt.262) 641 at 705, B-C
120. Balonwu v. Chinyelu (1991) 4 NWLR (Pt.183) 30 at 40, G
121. Balonwu v. Chinyelu (1991) 4 NWLR (Pt.183) 30 at 41, B (quoting with approval the trial judge)
122. Balonwu v. Obi (2007) 5 NWLR (Pt.1028) 488 at 563, B
123. Bamgboye v. Olarewaju (1991) 4 NWLR (Pt.184) 132 at 151, G
124. Bamidele v. Commissioner for Local Govt & Community Dev., Lagos State (1994) 2 NWLR (Pt.328) 568 at 586, D
125. Basheer v. Same (1992) 4 NWLR (Pt.236) 491 at 507, E-F
126. Bayero v. Mainasara & Sons Ltd (2006) 8 NWLR (Pt.982) 391 at 423, D
127. Bedding Holdings Ltd v. National Electrical Comm. (1992) 8 NWLR (Pt. 260) 428 at 437-438, H-A
128. Bello v. C.O.P (2018) 2 NWLR (Pt.1603) 262 at 285; 323, D-F
129. Bello v. Governor of Gombe State (2016) 8 NWLR (Pt.1514) 219 at 291-292 G-C
130. Bello v. Otolorin (1996) 9 NWLR (Pt.470) 49 at 72, C-D quoting himself in the unreported case CA/I/14/92 Madam

List of Cases in Alphabetical Order

Asiawu Adeteju Korede v. Prince Adebayo Adedokun & Another delivered on 20th June, 1994.

131. Bille v. State (2016) 15 NWLR (Pt.1536) 363 at 390, B-D
132. Braithwaite v. Dalhatu (2016) 13 NWLR (Pt.1528) 32 at 57 E-G
133. Broad Bank of Nig. Ltd v. Olayiwola (2005) 3 NWLR (Pt. 912) 434 at 457, H
134. Broad Bank of Nig. Ltd v. Olayiwola (2005) 3 NWLR (Pt.912) 434 at 458, H
135. Buhari v. Obasanjo (2005) 13 NWLR (Pt. 941) 1 at 281, B
136. Buhari v. Obasanjo (2005) 13 NWLR (Pt. 941) 1 at 294, F
137. Buhari v. Obasanjo (2005) 13 NWLR (Pt. 941) 1 at 300, D
138. Bulet Int'l (Nig.) Ltd v. Olaniyi (2017) 17 NWLR (Pt.1594) 260 at 294, D-E
139. Busari v. Oseni (1992) 4 NWLR (Pt.237) 557 at 592, B-C
140. C & C Const. Co. Ltd v. Okhai (2003) 18 NWLR (Pt.851) 79 at 100, E
141. Camptel Int'l SPA v. Dexson Ltd (1996) 7 NWLR (Pt.459) 170 at 191, B-C
142. Carribbean Trading & Fidelity Corp. v. NNPC (1992) 7 NWLR (Pt.252) 161 at 182, H
143. Ceekay Traders v. General Motors Co. Ltd. (1992) 2 NWLR (Pt.222)132 at 162, D
144. Chevron (Nig.) Ltd v. Onwugbelu (1996) 3 NWLR (Pt.437) 404 at 417, G
145. Chevron (Nig.) Ltd v. Onwugbelu (1996) 3 NWLR (Pt.437) 404 at 419D quoting the Supreme Court in The State v. Gwanto (1983) 3 SC 62 at 76
146. Chevron (Nig.) Ltd v. Onwugbelu (1996) 3 NWLR (Pt.437) 404 at 419, G
147. Chime v. Ude (1996) 7 NWLR (Pt. 461) 379 at 446, C (in his dissenting opinion)

148. Chinemelu v. C.O.P. (1995) 4 NWLR (Pt.390) 467 at 483, D
149. Chinemelu v. C.O.P. (1995) 4 NWLR (Pt.390) 467 at 483, E
150. Chinwendu v. Mbamali (1980) 3 to 4 SC 31 at 80-81
151. Chiwendu v. Mbamali (1980) 3/4 S.C. 31 at 81-82
152. Chrisray (Nig) Ltd v. Elson & Neil Ltd (1990) 3 NWLR (Pt.140) 630 at 641, G
153. Chukwu Const. Co. Ltd v. Uwechia (2000) 2 NWLR (Pt. 643) 92 at 99, F
154. Chukwuma v. Chukwuma (1996) 1 NWLR (Pt.426) 543 at 553, E-F
155. Citee Int'l Estates Ltd v. Francis (2014) 8 NWLR (Pt.1408) 139 at 159, C-D
156. Cocoa Merchant Ltd v. Commodities Sales Ltd (1993) 1 NWLR (Pt.271) 627 at 637, D
157. Coker v. Adetayo (1992) 6 NWLR (Pt.249) 612 at 625, G-H
158. Compt. Nig. Prison Service v. Adekanye (1999) 6 NWLR (Pt. 607) 381 at 388, G-H
159. Compt. Nig. Prison Service v. Adekanye (1999) 6 NWLR (Pt.607) 381 at 388, G-H
160. Comptroller of Nigeria Prisons v. Adekanye (1999) 10 NWLR (Pt.623) 400 at 421, G-H
161. Credit Alliance Finance Services Ltd v. Mallah (1998) 10 NWLR (Pt. 569) 341 at 351, C-D
162. Dahuwa v. Adeniran (1993) 2 NWLR (Pt.277) 580 at 287, F
163. Daily Times (Nig.) Plc v. Magoro (2000) 15 NWLR (Pt.692) 855 at 867, B
164. Daniang v Teachers Service Commission (1996) 5 NWLR (Pt.446) 96 at 109, B-C
165. Daniel v. F.R.N (2014) 8 NWLR (Pt.1410) 570 at 617 paras. A - D
166. Dantata & Sawoe Const. v. Egbe (1993)4 NWLR (Pt.287) 335 at 345, E

List of Cases in Alphabetical Order

167. Dapianlong v. Dariye (2007) 8 NWLR (Pt.1036) 332 at 415-416, H-C
168. Darma v. Oceanic Bank Int'l (Nig.) Ltd (2005) 4 NWLR (Pt.915) 391 at 408, E
169. Dibie v. State (2007) 9 NWLR (Pt.1038) 30 at 57, G
170. Din v. African Newspapers Ltd (1990) 3 NWLR (Pt.139) 392 at 408-409, H-A
171. Doma v. Ogiri (1998) 3 NWLR (Pt.541) 246 at 269, B-D
172. Dugeri v. Vee-Networks Ltd (2015) 2 NWLR (Pt.1442) 30 at 49 paras. D-E
173. Ebhodaghe v. Okoye (2004) 18 NWLR (Pt.905) 472 at 495, C-D
174. Edet v. Chief of Air Staff (1994) 2 NWLR (Pt.324) 41 at 61, B quoting Grotius, the great philosopher jurist.
175. Edet v. Chief of Staff (1994) 2 NWLR (Pt. 324) 41 at 60E-F quoting Halsbury's Laws of England, 4thEdition (Vol.1) at p. 80 para 66
176. Edozien v. Edozien (1993) 1 NWLR (Pt.272) 678 at 693, D
177. Effiom v State (1995) 1 NWLR (Pt.373) 507 at 622, C
178. Effiom v. State (1995) 1 NWLR (Pt.373) 507 at 519, E-F
179. Effiom v. State (1995) 1 NWLR (Pt.373) 507 at 578, B
180. Effiom v. State (1995) 1 NWLR (Pt.373) 507 at 585, C-D
181. Effiom v. State (1995) 1 NWLR (Pt.373) 507 at 617, C
182. Effiong v. State (2017) 2 NWLR (Pt.1549) 205 at 230, paras. F-G
183. Egbe v. Adefarasin (1985) 1 NWLR (Pt.3) 549 at 567, G
184. Egbe v. Yusuf (1992) 6 NWLR (Pt. 245) 1 at 19, E
185. Egbo v. Agbara (1997) 1 NWLR (Pt.481) 293 at 315, F
186. Egbuo v. Chukwu (1998) 10 NWLR (Pt.570) 499 at 510, paras. B-D
187. Ejabulor v. Osha (1990) 5 NWLR (Pt.148) 1 at 14, E-F
188. Ejimkonye v. State (2000) 3 NWLR (Pt.648) 262 at 272, E-F

189. Ejimkonye v. State (2000) 3 NWLR (Pt.648) 262 at 273, E-F
190. Ekanem v. Akpan (1991) 8 NWLR (Pt.211) 616 at 634, B quoting a restatement of the duties counsel owes to the court in Rondel v. W (1966) 3. All ER 657/665-668
191. Eleran v. Aderonpe (2008) 11 NWLR (Pt.1097) 50 at 79 paras. F-G
192. Elias v. Elias (2001) 9 NWLR (Pt.718) 429 at pages 445-446, H-A
193. Elochin (Nig.) Ltd v. Mbadiwe (1986) 1 NWLR (Pt.14) 47 at 60
194. Emerah v. Chiekwe (1996) 7 NWLR (Pt.462) 536 at 548, A-B
195. Emerah v. Chiekwe (1996) 7 NWLR (Pt.462) 536 at 548, D-E
196. Emesim v. Nwachukwu (1999) 6 NWLR (Pt.605) 154 at 169, D
197. Emesim v. Nwachukwu (1999) 6 NWLR (Pt.605) 154 at 169, E
198. Emodi v. Kwentoh (1996) 2 NWLR (Pt.433) 656 at 681, E-F
199. Enigwe v. Akaigwe (1992) 2 NWLR (Pt.225) 505 at 531, para H
200. Enigwe v. Akaigwe (1992) 2 NWLR (Pt.225) 505 at 535-536, H-A
201. Enigwe v. Akaigwe (1992) 2 NWLR (Pt.225) 505 at 536B (quoting former Chief Justice of India in Behram Khurshid Pesikaka v. Bombay State (1955) AIR 42 at 123
202. Equity Bank (Nig.) Ltd v. Daura (1999) 10 NWLR (Pt.621) 147 at 159, E
203. Eribuna v. Obiorah (1999) 8 NWLR (Pt.616) 622 at 643, F
204. Eribuna v. Obiorah (1999) 8 NWLR (Pt.616) 622 at 645, C
205. Erisi v. Idika (No.1) (1987) 4 NWLR (Pt.66) 503
206. Eseigbe v. Agholor (1993) 9 NWLR (Pt.316) 128 at 141-142, H-A

List of Cases in Alphabetical Order

207. Eti-Osa Local Govt v. Jegede (2007) 10 NWLR (Pt.1043) 537 at 558, F-G
208. Eti-Osa Local Govt v. Jegede (2007) 10 NWLR (Pt.1043) 537 at 559, B
209. Eyibagbe v. Eyibagbe (1996) 1 NWLR (Pt.425) 408 at 415, D
210. Ezegbu v. FATB Ltd (1992) 1 NWLR (Pt.216) 197 at 206, E-F
211. Ezeugo v. Ohanyere (1978) 6-7 SC 171 at 184, para.30
212. Fame Publication Ltd v. Encomium Ventures Ltd (2000) 8 NWLR (Pt. 667) 105 at 111, D-E
213. Fasehun v. A.-G., Federation (2006) 6 NWLR (Pt.975) 141 at 153-154, H-A
214. Fawehinmi v. NBA (No.2) (1989) NWLR (Pt.105) 558 at 627
215. Fawhinmi v. Akilu (1994) 6 NWLR (Pt.351) 387 at 474, B-C
216. Fawhinmi v. Akilu (1994) 6 NWLR (Pt.351) 387 at 474, D
217. FBN Plc v. Ejikeme (1996) 7 NWLR (Pt.462) 597 at 616, A-B
218. FBN Plc v. Ejikeme (1996) 7 NWLR (Pt.462) 597 at 616, B
219. FDB Financial Services Ltd v. Adesola (2000) 8 NWLR (Pt. 668) 170 at 182, G-H
220. Finnih v. Imade (1992) 1 NWLR (Pt.219) 511 at 537, E-F
221. Finnih v. Imade (1992) 1 NWLR (Pt.219) 511 at 542, C-D
222. FIPDC (Nig.) Ltd v. EAS Ltd (2006) 6 NWLR (Pt.975) 1 at 25, H-A
223. First Fuels Ltd v. NNPC (2007) 2 NWLR (Pt.1018) 276 at 301, C-D
224. Folarin v. State (1995) 1 NWLR (Pt.371) 313 at 323, C
225. Folarin v. State (1995) 1 NWLR (Pt.371) 313 at 323, F-G quoting Brett, F.J. in Latifu Gbadamosi v. Queen (1959) 4 FSC 181 at 183
226. Folorunsho v. Folorunsho (1996) 5 NWLR (Pt.450) 612 at 620, G-H

227. Fumudoh v. Aboro (1991) 9 NWLR (Pt.214) 210 at 231, A
228. G. Adamawa State v. A. G. Fed. (2005) 18 NWLR (Pt.958) 581 at 654 paras B-C
229. Galadima v. Tambai (2000) 11 NWLR (Pt.677) 1 at 15, E, F and G
230. Garba v. Federal Civil Service Commission (1988) 19 NSCC (Pt.1) 306 at 320
231. Gbadamosi v. Dairo (2007) 3 NWLR (Pt.1021) 282 at 306, A-B
232. Globe Motors Holdings Ltd v. Honda Motor Co. Ltd (1998) 5 NWLR (Pt.550) 373 at 381, F
233. Gomes v. Punch (Nig.) Ltd (1999) 5 NWLR (Pt.602) 303 at 311 - 312
234. Gomwalk v. Okwuosa (1996) 3 NWLR (Pt.439) 681 at 691, G-H
235. Governor of Ekiti State v. Ojo (2006) 17 NWLR (Pt.1007) 95 at 129, B
236. Governor of Lagos State v. Ojukwu (1986) 1 NWLR (Pt.18) 621 at 634, F
237. Governor of Lagos State v. Ojukwu (1986) 1 NWLR (Pt.18) 621 at 636, C-D
238. Governor of Lagos State v. Ojukwu (1986) 1 NWLR (Pt.18) 621 at 638, E-F
239. Green v. Green (1987) NSCC (Vol. 18) 1115 at 1143, 48-51
240. Greenbelt Ref. Ltd v. FBN Plc (1996) 6 NWLR (Pt.455) 502 at 506, G
241. Guardian Newspaper Ltd v. A.G. Federation (1995) 5 NWLR (Pt. 398) 703 at 738, F-G quoting Professor Ogwurike in his book titled "Concept of Law in English Speaking Africa" at page 194
242. Guardian Newspaper Ltd v. A.G. Federation (1995) 5 NWLR (Pt.398) 703 at 753, C-D

List of Cases in Alphabetical Order

243. Guardian Newspaper Ltd v. A.G. Federation (1995) 5 NWLR (Pt.398) 703 at 738-739, H-A
244. Guardian Newspaper Ltd v. A.-G., Federation (1995) 5 NWLR (Pt.398) 703 at 752, C
245. Guardian Newspaper Ltd v. A.-G., Federation (1995) 5 NWLR (Pt.398) 703 at 738, H quoting Professor Ogwurike in his book titled "Concept of Law in English Speaking Africa" at page 194
246. Guardian Newspaper Ltd. v. A.G. Federation (1995) 5 NWLR (Pt.398) 703 at 737-738, H-D quoting Mr. Justice Brandels in Whitney v. California 274 US 367 89 Guardian Newspaper Ltd v. A.-G., Federation (1995) 5 NWLR (Pt. 398) 703 at 752, C
247. Guinness (Nig.) Ltd v. Udeani (2000) 14 NWLR (Pt.687) 367 at 391, G-C
248. Guinness (Nig.) Ltd v. Udeani (2000) 14 NWLR (Pt.687) 367 at 395, C
249. Guinness (Nig.) Ltd v. Udeani (2000) 14 NWLR (Pt.687) 367 at 395, C
250. Guinness Nig. Plc v. Nwoke (2000) 15 NWLR (Pt.689) 135 at 150, C
251. Hallmark Bank Ltd v. Akaluso (1995) 5 NWLR (Pt.395) 306 at 313, G
252. Hayaki v. Dogara (1993) 8 NWLR (Pt.313) 586 at 598, G
253. Hayes v. Hayes (2000) 3 NWLR (Pt.648) 276 at 294, G-H
254. Houtmangracht v. Oduba (1995) 1 NWLR (Pt.371) 295 at 311 C, quoting Friedrich Von Savigny
255. Houtmangracht v. Oduba (1995) 1 NWLR (Pt.371) 295 at 311, B-C
256. Houtmangracht v. Oduba (1995) 1 NWLR (Pt.371) 295 at 311, D

257. Houtmangracht v. Oduba (1995) 1 NWLR (Pt.371) 295 at 311, E
258. Houtmangracht v. Oduba (1995) 1 NWLR (Pt.371) 295 at 311, E-F
259. Ibid at 562, B-C
260. Ibrahim v. Emein (1996) 2 NWLR (Pt.430) 322 at 333, F-G
261. Ibrahim v. Emein (1996) 2 NWLR (Pt.430) 322 at 337, B
262. Ibrahim v. Emein (1996) 2 NWLR (Pt.430) 322 at 337, C
263. Ibrahim v. Emein (1996) 2 NWLR (Pt.430) 322 at 337, G-H
264. Ibrahim v. State (1995) 3 NWLR (Pt.381) 35 at 48, E-F
265. Ibrahim v. State (1995) 3 NWLR (Pt.381) 35 at 48, F-G
266. Ibrahim v. The State (1995) 3 NWLR (Pt.381) 35 at 48, E-F
267. Ichi v. State (1996) 9 NWLR (Pt.470) 83 at 90, H
268. Ikpana v. RTPCN (2006) 3 NWLR (Pt. 966) 106 at 134, C-D
269. Ilori v. Benson (2000) 9 NWLR (Pt. 673) 570 at 579, G-H
270. Imah v. Okogbe (1993) 9 NWLR (Pt.316) 159 at 173, D-E
271. IMNL v. Nwachukwu (2004) 13 NWLR (Pt.891) 543 at 570-571, H-A
272. INEC v. Musa (2003) 3 NWLR (Pt.806) 72 at 214, G-H
273. Isamade v. Okei (1998) 2 NWLR (Pt.538) 455 at 468, B-C
274. ISC Services Ltd. v. G.C. Ltd. (2006) 6 NWLR (Pt. 977) 481 at 510 paras. A-D
275. Isheno v. Julius Berger (Nig) Plc. (2008) 6 NWLR (Pt.1084) 582 at 602-603, H-B
276. Iwuno v. Dieli (1990) 5 NWLR (Pt.149) 126 at 134, H
277. Iwuno v. Dieli (1990) 5 NWLR (Pt.149) 126 at 134-135, H-B
278. J.B. Estate Development & Properties Ltd v. Nzegwu (N0.2) (2016) 6 NWLR (Pt.1507) 117 at 158, G-H
279. J.B. Estate Development & Properties Ltd v. Nzegwu (No.2) (2016) 6 NWLR (Pt.1507) 137 at 158, A-B
280. Jamin Systems Consultants Ltd v. Braithwaite (1996) 5 NWLR (Pt.449) 459 at 470, B-C

List of Cases in Alphabetical Order

281. Jamin Systems Consultants Ltd v. Braithwaite (1996) 5 NWLR (Pt.449) 459 at 470, C
282. Josiah v. The State (1985) 1 NWLR (Pt.1) 125 at 141, G-H
283. Jukok Int'l v. Diamond Bank Plc. (2016) 6 NWLR (Pt.1507) 55 at 80;115, A-B
284. Kaduna Textiles Ltd v. Umar (1994) 1 NWLR (Pt.319) 143 at 159, G
285. Kajubo v. State (1988) 1 NWLR (Pt.73)721 at 738, G
286. Kalango v. Governor of Bayelsa (2002) 17 NWLR (Pt.617) at page 633-634, H-A
287. Katto v. CBN (1991) 9 NWLR (Pt.214) 126 at 145, G-H
288. Kolo v. C.O.P. (2017) 9 NWLR (Pt.1569) 118 at 157-158, D-C
289. Kotoye v. Saraki (1995) 6 NWLR (Pt.402) 504 at 508, G-H
290. Kurfi v. Mohammed (1993) 2 NWLR (Pt.277) 602 at 619, F-H
291. Kwajaffa v. BON Ltd (2004) 13 NWLR (Pt.889) 146 at page 183, E-H
292. Ladoja v. INEC (2007) 12 NWLR (Pt. 1017) 119 at 187, H-A
293. Ladoja v. INEC (2007) 12 NWLR (Pt.1047) 115 at 189, paras. C-D
294. Ladoja v. INEC (2007) 12 NWLR (Pt.1047) at 115. Referred to by Mohammad, J.S.C - Nyako v. A.S.H.A. (2017) 6 NWLR (Pt.1562) 347 at 400, A-B
295. Lau v P.D.P 4 NWLR (2018) 6 NWLR (Pt.1608) 60 at 128, H-A
296. Lau v. P.D.P (2018) 4 NWLR (Pt.1608) 123 at paras. E-F
297. Lau v. P.D.P 4 NWLR (2018) 6 NWLR (Pt.1608) 60 at127, D-E
298. Lenas Fibreglass Ltd v. Furtado (1997) 5 NWLR (Pt.504) 220 at 236, C
299. Lokpobiri v. Ogola (2016) 3 NWLR (Pt.1499) at 370 paras. F-G
300. Lokpobiri v. Ogola (2016) 3 NWLR (Pt.1499) at 372 para C

301. Lokpobiri v. Ogola (2016) 3 NWLR (Pt.1499) at 384 paras. D-G
302. LSDPC v. Nig. Land and See Foods Ltd (1992) 5 NWLR (Pt.244) 653 at 673, A
303. Macaulay v. RZB of Austria (1999) 4 NWLR (Pt. 600) 599 at 611-612, H-A
304. Madike v. State (1992) 8 NWLR (Pt.257) 85 at 103, D
305. Madu v. Okeke (1998) 5 NWLR (Pt.548) 159 at 164, E-F
306. Maersk Line v. Addide Investment Ltd (2002) 11 NWLR (Pt.778) 317 at 383, B-C
307. Maideribe v. FRN (2014) 5 NWLR (Pt. 1399) 68 at 99-100 paras H-A
308. Makarfi v. Poroye (2017) 10 NWLR (Pt.1574) 419 at 440-441; 425, G-D
309. Mba v. Mba (1999) 10 NWLR (Pt.623) 503 at 513, D
310. Mbanefo v. Molokwu (2014) 6 NWLR (Pt.1403) 377 at 416-417 paras. H- B
311. Menakaya v. Menakaya (1996) 9 NWLR (Pt.472) 256 at 304, G-H
312. Menkita v. Menkita (2000) 8 NWLR (Pt.667) 154 at 169, A-B
313. Merotohun v. State (1992) 7 NWLR (Pt.254) 443 at 451, F
314. MHWUN v. Minister of Labour & Productivity (2005) 17 NWLR (Pt.953) 120 at 147, G-H
315. Mil. Admin, Delta State v. Olu of Warri (1997) 7 NWLR (Pt.513) 430 at 466-467 H-A
316. Military Governor of Lagos State v. Ojukwu (1986) 2 SC 277 at 298-299
317. Moghalu v. Ngige (2005) 4 NWLR (Pt.914) 1 at 32, E-F
318. Mojekwu v. Mojekwu (1997) 7 NWLR (Pt.512) 283 at 305, A-B

List of Cases in Alphabetical Order

319. Mojekwu v. Mojekwu (1997) 7 NWLR (Pt.512) 283 at 305, B-C
320. Mueller v. Mueller (2006) 6 NWLR (Pt.977) 627 at 645 paras. F-G
321. Muhammed v. A.B.U., Zaria (2014) 7 NWLR (Pt.1407) at 531, para. B
322. Muhammed v. A.B.U., Zaria (2014) 7 NWLR (Pt.1407) at 531, paras. D-E
323. Musa v. INEC (2002) 11 NWLR (Pt.778) 223 at 309-310 paras. F-B
324. M.V. Lopex v. N.O.C. & S. Ltd. (2003) 15 NWLR (Pt.844) at 488, paras. F-G
325. N I M B Ltd. v. U B N (2004) 12 NWLR (Pt.888) 599 at 619 paras. E-F
326. N.A.A. v. Orjiakor (1998) 6 NWLR (Pt.553) 265 at 277-278, A-H
327. N.I.O. & M. R. v. Okonya (1996) 4 NWLR (Pt.444) 611 at 620 para. H
328. N.I.O. & M. R. v. Okonya (1996) 4 NWLR (Pt.444) 611 at620 paras. F-G
329. Nafiu Rabiu v. The State (1981) 2 NCLR 293 at 326.
330. National Bank of Nig. Ltd v. Opeola (1994) 1 NWLR (Pt.319) 126 at 141, H
331. NBCI v. MGI Co. Ltd (1992) 2 NWLR (Pt.221) 71 at 85, D
332. Ndiwe v. Shingleton& Co. Ltd (1993) 2 NWLR (Pt. 274) 242 at 250, D-E quoting Eso, J.S.C. who quoted Lord Scarman in Sodipo v. Lemminkainen OY (No.1) (1986) 1 S.C. 197 at 217
333. Ndiwe v. Shinleton & Co. Ltd (1993) 2 NWLR (Pt.274) 242 at 250, C-D quoting Eso, J.S.C.in Sodipo v. Lemminkainen OY (No.1) (1986) 1 S.C. 197 at 217.
334. NDLEA v. Okorodudu (1997) 3 NWLR (Pt.492) 221 at 247, C

335. Ndokwu v. LPDC (2007) 5 NWLR (Pt.1026) 1 at 48, E
336. Ndoma-Egba v. Govt., Cross River State (1991) 4 NWLR (Pt.188) 773 at 789, H
337. NEC v. Nzeribe (1991) 5 NWLR (Pt.192) 458 at 470 F quoting Lord Atkins's dictum in Liversidge v. Anderson (1948), AC 206
338. NH International SA v. NHH Limited (2007) 7 NWLR (Pt.1032) 86 at 114, G
339. NIC v. Acen Insurance Co. Ltd & 92 Ors (2007) 6 NWLR (Pt.1031) 589 at 600, F
340. Nigerian Air Force v. Kalmaldeen (2007) 7 NWLR (Pt.1032) 164 at 190, D
341. Nipol Ltd v. Bioku Invest. & Property Co. Ltd (1992) 3 NWLR (Pt.232) 727 at 753, D-E
342. NITEL Plc v. Rockonoh Property Co. Ltd (1995) 2 NWLR (Pt. 378) 473 at 496, G-H
343. NITEL Plc v. Rockonoh Property Co. Ltd (1995) 2 NWLR (Pt.378) 473 at 512, A
344. NITEL Plc v. Rockonoh Property Co. Ltd. (1995) 2 NWLR (Pt.378) 473 at 512, A
345. Nnamani v. Nnaji (1999) 7 NWLR (Pt. 610) 313 at 334 paras D-E
346. Nnamani v. Nnaji (1999) 7 NWLR (Pt. 610) 313 at 334 paras D-E
347. Nnodim v. Amadi (1993) 1 NWLR (Pt.271) 568 at 584, H
348. NTA v. Babatope (1996) 4 NWLR (Pt.440) 75 at 90, G-H
349. NTA v. Babatope (1996) 4 NWLR (Pt.440) 75 at 94, B-C
350. Ntuks v. Nigerian Ports Authority (2000) 4 NWLR (Pt. 654) 639 at 650, C
351. Nwadiaro v. Shell Dev. Co. Ltd (1990) 5 NWLR (Pt.150) 322 at 335, G

List of Cases in Alphabetical Order

352. Nwadiaro v. Shell Dev. Co. Ltd (1990) 5 NWLR (Pt.150) 322 at 336, A
353. Nwagbogu v. Abadom (1994) 7 NWLR (Pt.356) 357 at 376-377 H-A quoting Lord Scarman in Choo v. Canden Islington Area Health Authority (1979) 2 All E.R. 910
354. Nwaigwe v. Okere (2008) 13 NWLR (Pt.1105) 445 at 479, C-D
355. Nwankwo v. State (1985) NCLR 228 at 297
356. Nwankwo v. State (1990) 2 NWLR (Pt.134) 627 at 637, G quoting Lord Green in Yuill v. Yuill (1945) 1 All ER 185
357. Nwokoro v. Nwosu (1990) 1 NWLR (Pt.129) 679 at 684, E
358. Nwokoro v. Onuma (1990) 3 NWLR (Pt.136) 22 at 35, H
359. Nwosu v. Imo State Environmental Sanitation Authority (1990) 2 NWLR (Pt.135) 688 at 717, F-G
360. Nwosu v. Minister of Housing (2005) 11 NWLR (Pt. 937) 441 at 459, G
361. Nwosu v. Minister of Housing (2005) 11 NWLR (Pt.937) 441 at 457, H
362. Nwosu v. Uche (2005) 17 NWLR (Pt. 955) 574 at 590, G-H
363. Nwosu v. Uche (2005) 17 NWLR (Pt.955) 574 at 595 C, F-G
364. Nwude v. F.R.N. (2016) 5 NWLR (Pt.1506) 471 at 515, A-B
365. Nyagba v. Mbanan (1996) 9 NWLR (Pt.471) 207 at 221, F quoting Oputa, J.S.C.in Overseas Construction Ltd v. Creek Enterprise Ltd (1985) 3 NWLR (Pt.13) 407 at 419.
366. Nyako v. A.S.H.A. (2017) 6 NWLR (Pt.1562) 347 at 412, paras. F-G
367. Nyako v. A.S.H.A. (2017) 6 NWLR (Pt.1562) 347, at 403 paras. E-F; H See also: Ajide v. Kelani (1985) 3 NWLR (Pt.12) page 248
368. Nyako v. A.S.H.A. (2017) 6 NWLR (Pt.1562) at 404-405, paras. H-A

369. Obasi Bros Co. Ltd v. MBAS Ltd (2005) 9 NWLR (Pt.929) 117 at pages 133, H and 134, D
370. Obeta v. Okpe (1996) 9 NWLR (Pt.473) 401 at 456, B-C
371. Obeta v. Okpe (1996) 9 NWLR (Pt.473) 401 at 456, G
372. Odessa v. FRN (No.2) (2005) 10 NWLR (Pt.934) 518 at 559, A-C
373. Odock v. State (2007) 7 NWLR (Pt.1033) 369 at 399, D and F
374. Odogwu v. Odogwu (1992) 2 NWLR (Pt.225) 539 at 558, H
375. Odogwu v. Odogwu (1992) 2 NWLR (Pt.225) 539 at 559, H-A
376. Odogwu v. Odogwu (1994) 1 NWLR (Pt.323) 708 at 713, G-C
377. Odogwu v. Odogwu (1994) 1 NWLR (Pt.323) 708 at 716, D-E
378. Ogboru v. Okowa (2016) 11 NWLR (Pt. 1522) 84 at 122, paras. F-G
379. Ogbuego v. P.D.P 2016 4 NWLR (Pt.1503) 446 at 486 F-G
380. Ogedengbe v. State (2014) 12 NWLR (Pt.1421) at 384 paras. B-C
381. Oghor v. State (1990) 3 NWLR (Pt.139) 484 at 501, H quoting Aniagolu, J.S.C. in Nwosu v. The State (1986) 4 NWLR (Pt.35) 348 at 359.
382. Ogoja L.G. A. v. Offoboche (1996) 7 NWLR (Pt.458) 48 at 87F quoting Karibi-Whyte, J.S.C. in Egbe v. Adefarasin (1985) 1 NWLR (Pt.3) 549 at 569
383. Ogunleye v. Oni (1990) 2 NWLR (Pt.135) 745 at 772, C-D
384. Ohuka v. State (1988) 1 NWLR (Pt.72) 539 at 550, B
385. Ojiebge v. Ubani (1961) 2 NSCC 153 at 154
386. Ojuya v. Nzeogwu (1996) 1 NWLR (Pt. 427) 713 at 724, C
387. Okafor v. Lagos State Government (2017) 4 NWLR (Pt.1556) 404 at 442 C-D

List of Cases in Alphabetical Order

388. Okafor v. Lagos State Govt. (2017) 4 NWLR (Pt.1556) 405 at 442, paras. C-E
389. Okeke v. Nwokoye (1999) 13 NWLR (Pt. 635) 495 at 508, C-D
390. Okeke v. Nwokoye (1999) 13 NWLR (Pt.635) 495 at 509, D-E
391. Okeke v. Okoli (2000) 1 NWLR (Pt.642) 641 at 655, D
392. Okhae v. Governor, Bendel State (1990) 4 NWLR (Pt.144) 327 at 356D quoting Sir Udoma, J.S.C. in Rabiu v. The State (1980) 8-11 SC 130 at 148-149
393. Okike v. L.P.D.C. (2005) 15 NWLR (Pt. 949) 471 at 520 paras. F-H
394. Okike v. LPDC (2005) 15 NWLR (Pt.949) 471 at 518-519, H-A
395. Okino v. Obanebira (1999) 13 NWLR (Pt.636) 535 at 556, F-G
396. Okochi v. Animkwoi (2003) 18 NWLR (Pt. 851) 1 at 28, E
397. Okolo v. UBN Ltd (1998) 2 NWLR (Pt.539) 618 at 660, A
398. Okolo v. UBN Ltd. (1998) 2 NWLR (Pt.539) 618 at 661, A
399. Okoroafor v. The Misc. Offence Tribunal (1995) 4 NWLR (Pt.387) 59 at 77, H
400. Okoroafor v. The Miscellaneous Offences Tribunal (1995) 4 NWLR (Pt. 387) 59 at 78, G
401. Okoroafor v. The Miscellaneous Offences Tribunal (1995) 4 NWLR (Pt.387) 59 at 78, D
402. Okoroafor v. The Miscellaneous Offences Tribunal (1995) 4 NWLR (Pt.387) 59 at 78, H
403. Okoroafor v. The Miscellaneous Offences Tribunal (1995) 4 NWLR (Pt.387) 59 at 78, C quoting Hon. Justice Charles Hughes in an address delivered to American Bar Association published in ABA Journal, Sept. 1925

404. Okoroafor v. The Miscellaneous Offences Tribunal (1995) 4 NWLR (Pt.387) 59 at 81, H
405. Okoroafor v. The Miscellaneous Offences Tribunal (1995) 4 NWLR (Pt.387) 59 at 75, H-A
406. Okorocha v. PDP (2014) 7 NWLR (Pt.1406) 213 at 269 paras C-D
407. Okoroji v. Ngwu (1992) 9 NWLR (Pt. 263) 113 at 128, D
408. Okpala v. D.G., NCMM (1996)4 NWLR (Pt. 444) 585 at 594, G-H
409. Okpala v. Okpu (2003) 5 NWLR (Pt. 812) 183 at 215, H
410. Okpala v. Okpu (2003) 5 NWLR (Pt.812) 183 at 214, G-H
411. Okpala v. Okpu (2003) 5 NWLR (Pt.812) 183 at 214, H
412. Okpala v. Okpu (2003) 5 NWLR (Pt.812) 183 at 215, B-C
413. Okpe v. Fan Milk Plc (2017) 2 NWLR (Pt.1549) 282 at 310, F
414. Okpe v. Fan Milk Plc. (2017) 2 NWLR (Pt. 1549) 282 at 310, B-C
415. Okpe v. Fan Milk Plc. (2017) 2 NWLR (Pt.1549) 282 at 310-311, H-A
416. Okpokpo v. Uko (1997) 11 NWLR (Pt.527) 114 at 125, F-G
417. Okulaja v. Adefulu (1992) 5 NWLR (Pt.244) 752 at 766, F-G
418. Oladele v. Nigerian Army (2004) (Pt.868) 166 at 181, D-G
419. Olafisoye v. Fed. Rep. of Nigeria (2004) 4 NWLR (Pt.864) 580 at 654-655, H-A
420. Olaniyan v. Oyewole (2008) 5 NWLR (Pt.1079) 114 at 138 paras. E-F
421. Olaniyan v. Oyewole (2008) 5 NWLR (Pt.1079) 114 at 146 paras. A-B
422. Olaniyi v. Aroyehun (1991) 5 NWLR (Pt.194) 652 at 687, E
423. Olatunji v. FRN (2003) 3 NWLR (Pt.807) 406 at 424, H
424. Olawuyi v. Adeyemi (1990) 4 NWLR (Pt.147) 746 at 779, H
425. Oloba v. Akereja (1988) 7 SC (Pt.1) 1 at 11-12

426. Olumesan v. Ogundepo (1996) 2 NWLR (Pt. 433) 628 at 653, A
427. Olumesan v. Ogundepo (1996) 2 NWLR (Pt.433) 628 at 651, D quoting Fanz Holdings Ltd v. Mrs. Lamotte (1977) NNLR 163 at 168
428. Olumesan v. Ogundepo (1996) 2 NWLR (Pt.433) 628 at 653, F
429. Onagoruwa v. IGP (1991) 5 NWLR (Pt. 193) 593 at 646, G
430. Onagoruwa v. IGP (1991) 5 NWLR (Pt.193) 593 at 650 C-D
431. Onagoruwa v. IGP (1991) 5 NWLR (Pt.193) 593 at 650, B
432. Onibudo v. Akibu (1982) 7 SC 60 at 62
433. Onigbede v. Balogun (1998) 4 NWLR (Pt.545) 281 at 291, C
434. Ononuju v. State (2014) 8 NWLR (Pt.1409) 345 at 395 paras D-E
435. Onuchukwu v. State 1998) 4 NWLR (Pt.547) 576 at 592, E
436. Onuoha v. R.B. Okafor & Others (1983) 2 SCNLR at 259-260
437. Onwo v. Oko (1996) 6 NWLR (Pt. 456) 584 at 613, E
438. Onwo v. Oko (1996) 6 NWLR (Pt.456) 584 at 600, H
439. Onwo v. Oko (1996) 6 NWLR (Pt.456) 584 at 613, E
440. Onwo v. Oko (1996) 6 NWLR (Pt.456) 584 at 613, F-G
441. Onyekwuluje v. Animashaun (1996) 3 NWLR (Pt. 439) 637 at 644, G-H
442. Onyekwuluje v. Animashaun (1996) 3 NWLR (Pt.439) 637 at 644, G
443. Opara v. Chinda (1996) 2 NWLR (Pt.432) 527 at 538, A-B
444. Orakwute v. Agagwu (1996) 8 NWLR (Pt. 466) 359 at 376, G-H
445. Orakwute v. Agagwu (1996) 8 NWLR (Pt.466) 359 at 375, G
446. Orakwute v. Agagwu (1996) 8 NWLR (Pt.466) 359 at 375, H

447. Orakwute v. Agagwu (1996) 8 NWLR (Pt.466) 359 at 376 para. B
448. Orakwute v. Agagwu (1996) 8 NWLR (Pt.466) 359 at 376, H
449. Orakwute v. Agagwu (996) 8 NWLR (Pt.466) 359 at 376, B-C
450. Orugbo v Una (2002) 16 NWLR (Pt.792) 175 at 211-212, H-C
451. Osafile v. Odi (No.1) (1990) 3 NWLR (Pt.137) 130 at 155, C-D
452. Osho v. Foreign Fin. Corp. (1991) 4 NWLR (Pt.184) 157 at 202, E-F
453. Oshoboja v. Amuda (1992) 6 NWLR (Pt.250) 690 at 709, F-G
454. Osia v. Edjekpo (2001) 10 NWLR (Pt.720) 233 at page 248, D
455. Oteju v. Magma Maritime Services Ltd (2000) 1 NWLR (Pt.640) 270 at 342, D-E
456. Oteju v. Magma Maritime Services Ltd (2000) 1 NWLR (Pt.640) 270 at 346, A-B
457. Oteju v. Oluguna (1992) 8 NWLR (Pt.262) 752 at 767, B-C
458. Oteju v. Oluguna (1992) 8 NWLR (Pt.262) 752 at 767, F-G
459. Oteju v. Oluguna (1992) 8 NWLR (Pt.262) 752 at 770, C
460. Owena Bank (Nig.) Plc v. Adedeji (2000) 7 NWLR (Pt.666) 609 at 631, D-E
461. Oyakhare v. State (2005) 15 N.W.L.R. (Pt.947) 180 Paras. F-H
462. Oyefeso v. Omogbehin (1991) 4 NWLR (Pt.187) 596 at 614-615, H-A
463. Oyewunmi v. Ogunesan (1990) 3 NWLR (Pt.137) 182 at 207, E-F
464. Ozoana v. P.S.C. (1995) 4 NWLR (Pt.391) 629 at 639, A-B

465. P.A.N. v. Oje (1997) 11 NWLR (Pt.530) 625 at 636, C-D
466. Pabod Supplies Ltd v. Beredugo (1996) 5 NWLR (Pt. 448)304 at 330, E
467. PDP v. Abubakar (2007) 3 NWLR (Pt.1022) 515 at 547, D-F
468. Pelfaco Ltd v. W.A.O.S. Ltd (1997) 10 NWLR (Pt.524) 222 at 238, F
469. Peters v. Ashamu (1995) 4 NWLR (Pt.388) 206 at 222, B
470. PGSS, Ikachi v. Igbudu (2005) 12 NWLR (Pt. 940) 543 at 574, F-G
471. Phoenix Motors Ltd v. N.P.F.M.B. (1993) 1 NWLR (Pt.272) 718 at 730, E-F
472. Phoenix Motors Ltd v. N.P.F.M.B. (1993) 1 NWLR (Pt.272) 718 at 730, C
473. Plateau State v. A.G. Federation (2006) 3 NWLR (Pt.967) 346 at 419, H
474. Plateau State v. A.G. Federation (2006) 3 NWLR (Pt.967) 346 at 420, D
475. Plateau State v. A.-G., Federation (2006) 3 NWLR (Pt.967) 346 at 419, G-H
476. Plateau State v. A.G., Federation (2006) 3 NWLR (Pt.967) 346 at 419, G
477. Prince Abubakar & 22 Ors v. INEC &Ors. EPR Vol. 9 414 at 533 See Electronic Law
478. Princewill v. State (1994) 6 NWLR (Pt.353) 703 at 715, C
479. Princewill v. Usman (1990) 5 NWLR (Pt.150) 274 at 282, G-H
480. Princewill v. Usman (1990) 5 NWLR (Pt.150) 274 at 283, A-B
481. Princewill v. Usman (1990) 5 NWLR (Pt.150) 274 at 286, F-G
482. Progress Bank (Nig) Ltd v. Ugonna (Nig) Ltd (1996) 3 NWLR (Pt.435) 202 at 218, C

483. Rabiu v. State (2005) 7 NWLR (Pt.925) 491 at 507, G
484. Rafukka v. Kurfi (1996) 6 NWLR (Pt.453) 235 at 244-245, H-A
485. REAN Ltd v. Aswani Textiles Ltd (1991) 2 NWLR (Pt.176) 639 at 665, F-G
486. Reg. Trustees of Ifeloju v. Kuku (1991) 5 NWLR (Pt.189) 65 at 79, G-H
487. Registered Trustee of Amorc v. Awoniyi (1994) 7 NWLR (Pt.355) 154 at 19, G
488. Republic Bank Ltd v. CBN (1998) 13 NWLR (Pt.581) 306 at 332, E
489. Salako v. Williams (1998) 11 NWLR (Pt.547) 505 at 520, D-E
490. Salami v. Bunginimi (1998) 9 NWLR (Pt.565) 235 at 243 quoting Lord Penzance in Combe v. Edwards (1878) LR 34 PD 103 at 142
491. Salim v. Ifenkwe (1996) 5 NWLR (Pt. 450) 564 at 588, E-F
492. Salim v. Ifenkwe (1996) 5 NWLR (Pt.450) 564 at 585-586, H-A
493. Salim v. Ifenkwe (1996) 5 NWLR (Pt.450) 564 at 586, E
494. Salim v. Ifenkwe (1996) 5 NWLR (Pt.450) 564 at 586, E-F
495. Salim v. Ifenkwe (1996) 5 NWLR (Pt.450) 564 at 587, B
496. Salim v. Ifenkwe (1996) 5 NWLR (Pt.450) 564 at 587, B
497. SBN Ltd v. De Lluch (2004) 18 NWLR (Pt.905) 341 at 358, F-H
498. Schmidt v. Umanah (1997) 1 NWLR (Pt.479) 75 at 83, C
499. Seismograph Services v. Mark (1993) 7 NWLR (Pt.304) 203 at 215, H-A
500. Seriki v. Are (1999) 3 NWLR (Pt. 595) 469 at 480, F-G
501. Seriki v. Are (1999) 3 NWLR (Pt. 595) 469 at 481 paras E-F
502. Shalla v. State (2007) 18 NWLR (Pt.1066) 240 at pages 299, C-D

List of Cases in Alphabetical Order

503. Sirpi Alusteel Const. (Nig.) Ltd v. Snig (Nig.) Ltd (2000) 2 NWLR (Pt.644) 229 at 240, F-G
504. Sofekun v. Akinyemi (1980) 5-7 SC 1 at 25-26
505. SPD (Nig.) Ltd v. Arho-Joe (Nig.) Ltd. (2006) 3 NWLR (Pt.966) 172 at 193, A
506. Spiess v. Oni (2016) 14 NWLR (Pt.1532) at 275, B
507. State Civil Service Commission v. Alexius I. Buzugbe (1984) 7 SC 19
508. State v. Onagoruwa (1992) 2 NWLR (Pt.221) 33 at 58-59, H-A
509. Steel Bell (Nig.) Ltd. v. Govt. of Cross River State (1996) 3 NWLR (Pt.438) 571 at 589, H
510. Steel Bell (Nig.) Ltd. v. Govt. of Cross River State (1996) 3 NWLR (Pt.438) 571at 589, C-D
511. Steel Bell (Nig.) Ltd. v. Govt. of Cross River State (1996) 3 NWLR (Pt.438) 571 at 588, H quoting the dictum of Lord Denning in Padfield v. Minister of Agriculture Fisheries and Food (1968) AC 997
512. Tanko v. Caleb (1999) 8 NWLR (Pt.616) 606 at 611, A
513. Tell Communications Ltd v. Marwa (2006) 4 NWLR (Pt.970) 315 at 333, H
514. Terytex (Nig) Ltd v. Nigerian Ports Authority (1989) 1 NWLR (Pt.96) 229 at 236, G
515. The Secretary, Iwo Central L.G. v. Adio (2000) 8 NWLR (Pt.667) 115 at 153, B
516. Towoju v. Governor of Kwara State (2005) 324 at 350, C-D
517. Trans Bridge Co. Ltd v. Survey Inter'l Ltd (1986) 4 NWLR (Pt. 37) 576 at 598, B
518. TSA Ind. Ltd v. Abacus Merchant Bank Ltd (1996) 2 NWLR (Pt.430) 305 at 317, D
519. UBA Ltd v. Taan (1993) 4 NWLR (Pt.287) 368 at 381, D
520. UBA Plc v. Coker (1996) 4 NWLR (Pt.441) 239 at 247, G

521. UBA v. Onagoruwa (1996) 3 NWLR (Pt.439) 700 at 708, B
522. UBN Ltd v. Ayoola (1998) 11 NWLR (Pt.573) 338 at 343, G-H
523. UBN Ltd v. Ayoola (1998) 11 NWLR (Pt.573) 338 at 343, H
524. Udoh v. State (1994) 2 NWLR (Pt.329) 666 at 685, E-F
525. Ugba v. Suswam (2014) 14 NWLR (Pt.1427) 264 at 345 paras. C-D
526. Ugbodume v. Abiegbe (1991) 8 NWLR (Pt.209) 261 at 275
527. Ugwu v. Ararume (2007) 12 NWLR (Pt.1048) 367 at page 514, D-E
528. Ukachukwu v. Uzodinma (2007) 9 NWLR (Pt. 1938) 167 at 190-191, H-A
529. Ukwunnenyi v. State (1989) 4 NWLR (Pt.114) 131 at 149, A
530. Ukwunnenyi v. State (1989) 4 NWLR (Pt.114) 131 at 149, B
531. Ukwunnenyi v. State (1989) 4 NWLR (Pt.114) 131 at 156, D-E
532. Umagba v. Ogbe (1996) 8 NWLR (Pt.468) 621 at 626, E-F
533. UMTHMB v. Dawa (2001) 16 NWLR (Pt.739) 424 at 448 paras. E-G
534. Unifam Ind. Ltd v. Oceanic Bank Inter'l (Nig.) Ltd (2005) 3 NWLR (Pt.911) 83 at 97, E
535. University of Calabar v. Esiaga (1997) 4 NWLR (Pt.502) 719 at 746, B-C
536. University of Ilorin v. UBN PLC (2002) 3 NWLR (Pt.755) 626 at 646 paras. A-C
537. Ushae v. COP (2005) 11 NWLR (Pt. 937) 499 at 533-534, H-A quoting Lord Denning, MR in his book "The Family Story"
538. Ushae v. COP (2005) 11 NWLR (Pt.937) 499 at 524, H
539. Ushae v. COP (2005) 11NWLR (Pt. 937) 499 at 530, C-D
540. Ushae v. COP (2005) 11NWLR (Pt. 937) 499 at 535, B

List of Cases in Alphabetical Order

541. Usikaro v. Itsekiri Land Trustees (1991) 2 NWLR (Pt.172) 150 at 180D-E quoting Lord Denning in Allen v. Alfred McAlpine & Sons Ltd (1968) 2 QB 229/245, 377
542. Usiobaifo v. Usibaifo (2005) 3 NWLR (Pt. 913) 665 at 692, E-G
543. UTB Ltd v. Dol. Pharm. (Nig.) Ltd (2002) 8 NWLR (Pt.770) 726 at 751, E
544. Utih v. Onoyivwe (1991) 1NWLR (Pt.166) 166 at 206, A
545. Uwagba v. Fed. Republic of Nigeria (2000) 13 NWLR (Pt.684) at 251, E
546. Uwagba v. Federal Republic of Nigeria (2000) 13 NWLR (Pt.684) at 251, C (referring to the opinion of Irikefe, J.S.C. in Echeazu v. Commissioner of Police (1974) 2 SC 55 at 69-70
547. Uzoagba v. C.O.P. (2014) 5 NWLR (Pt.1401) 441 at 465 paras. D-F
548. Uzondu v. Uzondu (1997) 9 NWLR (Pt.521) 466 at page 483, E-F
549. Veritas Ins. Co. Ltd v. Citi Trust Inv. Ltd (1993) 3 NWLR (Pt.281) 349 at 369 F
550. Veritas Ins. Co. Ltd v. Citi Trust Inv. Ltd (1993) 3 NWLR (Pt.281) 349 at 369, G
551. Veritas Ins. Co. Ltd v. Citi Trust Inv. Ltd (1993) 3 NWLR (Pt.281) 349 at 367-368, H-A
552. Waniko v. Ade-John (1999) 8 NWLR (Pt.619) 401 at 410, C-D
553. Weide & Co. (Nig.) Ltd v. Weide & Co Hamburg (1992) 6 NWLR (Pt.249) 627 at 641
554. Wellington v. Regd. Trustees, Ijebu-Ode (2000) 3 NWLR (Pt.647) 130 at 139, D-E
555. Wema Bank Plc v. Abiodun (2006) 9 NWLR (Pt. 984) 1 at 32, H

556. Whyte v. Jack (1996) 2 NWLR (Pt.431) 407 at 441, H
557. Whyte v. Jack (1996) 2 NWLR (Pt.431) 407 at 449, B-C quoting from the book of Kayode Eso, J.S.C.- "Nigerian Grundnorm" at page 39
558. Williams v. Akintunde (1995) 3 NWLR (Pt.381) 101 at 114, G
559. Yakubu v. State (2007) 9 NWLR (Pt.1038) 1 at 19, E-F
560. Yusuf v. Obasanjo (2005) 18 NWLR (Pt.956) 96 at C-D
561. Yusufu v. Obasanjo (2003) 16 NWLR (Pt.847) 554 at 639, H
562. Yusufu v. Obasanjo (2003) 16 NWLR (Pt.847) 554 at 641, G
563. Zaboley Inter'l Ltd v. Omogbehin (2005) 17 NWLR (Pt.953) 200 at 223, G
564. Zimit v. Mahmoud (1993) 1 NWLR (Pt.267) 71 at 90, E
565. Zimit v. Mahmoud (1993) 1 NWLR (Pt.267) 71 at 91, E-F
566. Zubairu v. State (2015) 16 NWLR (Pt.1486) at 528, paras. D-F

INDEX

Abdul-Kadir, Abubakar Jega, J.C.A., 160
Abimbola Osarugue Obaseki-Adejumo, J.C.A., 169
Abubakar Bashir Wali, J.C.A., 114
Abubakar Bashir Wali, J.S.C., 134
Adolphus Godwin Karibi-Whyte, J.S.C, 7, 12, 15, 22, 63, 68, 79, 83
Adrian Chukwuemeka Orah, J.C.A., 77, 78
Akintola Olufemi Ejiwunmi, J.C.A., 3, 50, 79
Akintola, Olufemi Ejiwunmi, J.S.C., 90, 154
Aloma Mariam Mukhtar, J.C.A., 136
Aloma Mariam Mukhtar, J.S.C., 11, 35, 64
Aloysius Iyorgyer Katsina-Alu, J.C.A., 5, 114
Aloysius Iyorgyer Katsina-Alu, J.S.C., 140
Amina Adamu Augie, J.C.A., 45, 139, 171
Andrews Otutu Obaseki, J.S.C, 3, 10, 12, 13, 33, 41, 68, 70, 89, 119, 146
Anthony Ikechukwu Iguh, J.S.C., 53, 55, 72, 133, 176
Anthony Nnaemezie Aniagolu, J.S.C., 17, 102, 138, 145
Atinuke Ige, J.C.A., 23
Atinuke Omobonike Ige, J.C.A., 82, 127
Augustine Nnamani, J.S.C., 61, 79
Biobele Abraham Georgewill J.C.A., 4
Bode Rhodes-Vivour, J.C.A., 135, 174
Bode Rhodes-Vivour, J.S.C., 155, 165, 166, 174, 175
Braimah Amen Omosun, J.C.A., 8
Chidi Nwaoma Uwa, J.C.A., 32
Chima Centus Nweze J.S.C., 151
Chinwe Eugenia Iyizoba J.C.A., 117
Christopher Mitchell Chukwuma-Eneh, J.C.A., 35, 76, 77, 145
Chukwudifu Akunne Oputa, J.S.C., 15, 127, 130, 136, 141
Clara Bata Ogunbiyi, J.S.C., 10, 36, 59, 95, 105, 154
Dahiru Musdapher, J.C.A., 24, 36, 176
Dahiru Musdapher, J.S.C., 73
Dalhatu Adamu, J.C.A., 97, 119
Dattijo Muhammad, J.S.C, 86
Dauda Azaki, J.C.A., 137
Dennis Onyejife Edozie, J.C.A., 28, 65, 70, 97

Index

Denton-West, Sotonye, J.C.A., 159, 161
Ejembi Eko, J.S.C., 3
Emmanuel Obioma Ogwuegbu, J.S.C., 18, 133
Emmanuel Olayinka Ayoola, J.C.A., 25, 26, 49
Emmanuel Olayinka Ayoola, J.S.C., 122
Emmanuel Takon Ndoma-Egba, J.C.A., 90
Ephraim Omorose Ibukun Akpata, J.C.A., 9
Ephraim Omorose Ibukun Akpata, J.S.C., 47, 101, 175
Eugene Chukwuemeka Ubaezonu, J.C.A., 47, 51, 53, 82, 103, 119, 142
Francis Fedode Tabai, J.C.A., 139
Francis Fedode Tabai, J.S.C., 78, 101, 102
Francis Olisa Awogu, J.C.A., 16
Galinje, Paul Adamu, J.C.A., 174
George Adesola Oguntade, J.C.A., 6, 14, 16, 28, 44, 72, 82, 125, 128, 143, 145
Gertrude Ifunanya Udom-Azogu, J.C.A., 32
Helen Moronkeji Ogunwumiju, J.C.A., 24, 159, 174
Ibrahim Kolapo Sulu-Gambari, J.C.A., 6, 67, 131
Ibrahim Mohammed Musa Saulawa, J.C.A., 159
Ibrahim Tanko Muhammad, J.C.A., 19, 20, 23, 37, 136, 137
Ibrahim Tanko Muhammad, J.S.C., 4, 38, 42, 55, 113, 130
Idris Legbo Kutigi, J.S.C., 27, 73
Ignatius Chukwudi Pats-Acholonu, J.S.C., 138, 153
Ignatius Chukwudi Pats-Acholonu, J.C.A., 5, 15, 16, 17, 23, 25, 26, 41, 42, 45, 46, 51, 53, 59, 63, 64, 65, 67, 73, 74, 75, 78, 80, 81, 82, 83, 84, 85, 91, 96, 120, 121, 124, 127, 131, 132, 134, 135, 136, 137, 140, 146, 152, 176, 177
Ignatius Chukwudi Pats-Acholonu, J.S.C., 44, 47, 52, 75, 76, 77, 84, 90, 109, 139, 145, 165
Ignatius Igwe Agube, J.C.A., 172
Isa Ayo Salami, J.C.A., 10, 30, 33, 34, 46, 72, 106, 132, 142
Ita George Mbaba, J.C.A., 4
James Ogenyi Ogebe, J.C.A., 83
Jimi Olukayode Bada, J. C. A., 152
John Afolabi Fabiyi, J.C.A., 71, 76, 81, 91, 109, 175
John Iyang Okoro, J.C.A., 75
John Iyang Okoro, J.S.C., 165
Joseph Diekola Ogundare, J.C.A., 120
Joseph Jeremiah Umoren, J.C.A., 105
Joseph Olubunmi Kayode Oyewole, J.C.A., 159, 172
Kalgo, Umaru Atu, J.S.C., 153
Kayode Eso, J.S.C., 3, 19, 21, 34, 80, 118, 129, 138, 209
Kudirat Motonmori Olatokunbo Kekere-Ekun J.S.C., 59, 117, 155, 156
Kumai Bayang Aka'ahs, J.S.C., 152
Kumai Bayang Akaahs, J.C.A., 11
Mahmud Mohammed, J.C.A., 73, 140
Mahmud Mohammed, J.S.C., 48
Mahmud Muhammad, J.S.C., 124
Mary Peter-Odili, J.S.C., 165
Mary Ukaego Peter-Odili, J.C.A., 114

Mary Ukaego Peter-Odili, J.S.C., 154, 155, 175
Massaoud Abdulrahman Oredola, J.C.A., 117
Michael Ekundayo Ogundare, J.C.A., 142
Mohammed Bello, C.J.N., 6, 101, 126, 181
Mohammed Lawal Garba, J.C.A., 30, 36
Monica B. Dogban-Mensem, J.C.A., 30
Monica Bolna'an Dongban-Mensem, J.C.A., 92, 170
Moronkeji Omotayo Onalaja, J.C.A., 19, 41, 55, 80, 110, 123, 136
Muhammad Saifullahi Muntaka Coomassie, J.C.A., 113
Muhammadu Lawal Uwais, J.S.C., 29
Muhammed Bello, C.J.N., 73
Muntaka-Coomassie, Mohammed Saifullahi, J.C.A., 153
Musa Dattijo Muhammad, J.C.A., 32, 140, 146, 147, 170
Niki Tobi, J.C.A., 5, 6, 7, 9, 12, 13, 14, 18, 21, 28, 33, 43, 44, 45, 46, 48, 49, 50, 51, 52, 53, 54, 60, 61, 62, 63, 65, 66, 68, 69, 70, 71, 77, 78, 79, 83, 84, 85, 86, 91, 92, 96, 97, 104, 106, 118, 121, 122, 123, 125, 128, 129, 130, 131, 133, 134, 135, 137, 141, 143, 144, 146, 177
Niki Tobi, J.S.C, 36, 47, 66, 68, 71, 74, 75, 76, 80, 81, 95, 103, 105, 109, 118, 139, 140, 141, 151, 160, 161, 169, 170, 171, 177
Nwali Sylvester Ngwuta, J.S.C., 114, 117, 155, 169

Nzeako, Ifeyinwa Cecilia, J.C.A., 171
Okay Achike, J.C.A., 26, 27, 35, 48, 51, 52, 53, 61, 62, 64, 66, 103, 113, 120, 121, 142, 147
Okay Achike, J.S.C., 71, 106
Olajide Olatawura, J.S.C., 14, 16, 29, 44, 46, 60, 120, 121, 125, 132, 138
Oludade Oladapo Obadina, J.C.A., 17
Olufunlola Oyelola Adekeye, J.C.A., 27, 31, 42, 95
Olukayode Ariwoola, J.C.A., 113
Onyekachi Aja Otisi, J.C.A., 38
Owolabi Kolawole, J.C.A., 7, 41, 43, 45, 66, 125
Paul Kemdilim Nwokedi, J.S.C., 62
Philip Nnaemeka-Agu, J.S.C., 9, 13, 27, 33, 34, 68, 119, 132, 135, 143, 144
Pius Olayiwola Aderemi, J.C.A., 11, 22, 23, 24, 61, 70, 85, 90, 91, 95, 96, 118, 124, 126, 128, 130, 146, 147, 176
Pius Olayiwola Aderemi, J.S.C., 121, 166
Rabiu Danlami Muhammad, J.C.A., 61, 126
Raphael Olufemi Rowland, J.C.A., 6, 34, 104, 127, 128
Saka Adeyemi Ibiyeye, J.C.A., 41, 74
Salihu Modibbo Alfa Belgore, J.S.C., 8, 31, 32, 67, 96, 169, 173
Samson Odemwingie Uwaifo, J.C.A., 5, 20, 26, 50, 51, 64, 65, 67, 69, 71, 143, 144
Samson Odemwingie Uwaifo, J.S.C., 21, 103, 147

Sir Adetokunbo Ademola, C.J.N., 49
Sotonye Denton-West, J.C.A., 29, 31, 32, 34
Stanley Shenko Alagoa, J.C.A., 37, 170
Stanley Shenko Alagoa, J.S.C., 171
Sule Aremu Olagunju, J.C.A., 17, 21, 37, 75, 126, 141
Suleiman Galadima, J.C.A., 17, 34, 60, 105, 122
Sylvanus Adiewere Nsofor, J.C.A., 54, 103
Sylvester Umaru Onu, J.C.A., 7
Sylvester Umaru Onu, J.S.C., 15, 22, 49, 104
Theresa Ngolika Orji-Abadua, J.C.A., 37
Tijani Abdullahi, J.C.A., 74, 109
Tsammani, Haruna Simon, J.C.A., 172
Udo Udoma, J.S.C., 29
Umaru Abdullahi, J.C.A., 20, 124, 129
Uthman Mohammed, J.S.C., 31, 110, 126, 127
Uzo I. Ndukwe-Anyanwu, J.C.A., 59
Victor Aimepomo Oyeleye Omage, J.C.A., 35
Victor James Obanua Chigbue, J.C.A., 45, 69
Walter Samuel Nkanu Onnoghen, C.J.N., 59, 154
Walter Samuel Nkanu Onnoghen, J.C.A., 123, 173
Walter Samuel Nkanu Onnoghen, J.S.C., 102, 122, 156
Yekini Olayiwola Adio, J.S.C., 95, 137, 219

ABOUT THE AUTHOR

Honourable Justice Jumoke Olusola Pedro attended the prestigious University of Lagos Akoka, Nigeria where she finished with a 2nd Class Upper degree in Law in 1980. In July 1981, she was called to the Nigerian Bar to practice as a Barrister and Solicitor of the Supreme Court. She practiced briefly between 1982-1984 as a Legal Practitioner with a reputable firm Akin Olugbade & Co., after completing her N.Y.S.C as a legal officer with the Military Police Apapa Cantonment. In 1984, she joined the Lower Bench of the Lagos State Judiciary as a Magistrate. She was later appointed as Registrar of Titles in Lagos State and rose through the Bench to become a Chief Magistrate. In 1999, she was appointed the Chief Registrar of the High Court and served as the Probate Registrar, the Sheriff, the Tax Master, and the Official Receiver.

About the Author

In the year 2001, she was appointed a High Court Judge of Lagos State and has served in that capacity since then. She has worked in various divisions of the court, General Civil, Family and Probate, Commercial, Fast Track, Lands Division and once a designated Judge of Economic and Financial Crimes Commission Matters. Her varied experience has helped her in putting together this book to assist Legal Practitioners, Law students, and the Bench.

His Lordship is a Deaconess in Guiding Light Assembly and a Chancellor of the Church of Nigeria Anglican Communion.

She is a member of the National Association of Women Judges in Nigeria, and a member of Olave Baden-Powell Society.

She is also a member of the Chartered Institute of Arbitrators -England and a Certified Mediator.

His Lordship is married to HE Olufemi Pedro a former Deputy Governor of Lagos State and they are blessed with four children..

www.ingramcontent.com/pod-product-compliance
Lightning Source LLC
Chambersburg PA
CBHW030919180526
45163CB00002B/396